Christian Faith for Handing On

Christian Faith for
Handing On

HELEN OPPENHEIMER

 CASCADE *Books* • Eugene, Oregon

CHRISTIAN FAITH FOR HANDING ON

Cascade Books
An Imprint of Wipf and Stock Publishers
199 W. 8th Ave., Suite 3
Eugene, OR 97401

www.wipfandstock.com

ISBN 13: 978-1-62564-234-9

Cataloguing-in-Publication data:

Oppenheimer, Helen.

Christian faith for handing on / Helen Oppenheimer.

x + 162 pp. ; 23 cm. Includes bibliographical references and index.

ISBN 13: 978-1-62564-234-9

1. Christianity—Philosophy. 2. Theology—Doctrinal. I. Title.

BT40 O58 2013

Manufactured in the U.S.A.

With love to my grandchildren's children,
whether they can remember me or not.

Contents

Preface | ix

Part I: Believing

1   Terms of Reference | 3

2   Matter and More | 13

3   The Argument from Value | 19

4   Recalcitrant Reality | 26

5   The Project of Creation | 34

6   Question of Fact | 40

7   The Hypothesis of Faith | 47

8   Rational Inquiry | 53

9   Gospel Story | 61

Part II: Belonging

10   One Another | 73

11   God in Charge | 81

12   Christian Hope | 87

13   Is Anyone There? | 95

14   The Means of Grace | 103

Part III: Behaving

15   Values, Human and Divine | 113

16   The Way | 120

17   Compare and Contrast | 129

18   Mercy | 139

19   Continuing | 147

Bibliography | 153

Names Index | 157

Preface

I OWE WARM THANKS TO many people; and especially to my son-in-law, Ivo Mosley, for his generous encouragement and in particular for his kind energy in putting me in touch with Cascade Books. I am grateful to the Parish of St Martin de Grouville and the people who minister here and worship here. My husband Michael has backed up everything I do for more than sixty-six years. Many of the people to whom I owe a lot are no longer in this world to be thanked. They are part of the Communion of Saints, on whose shoulders Christians today are standing.

Philosophers approach questions by way of thinking them out and trying to analyze them, chewing at problems like a dog with a bone. This is the style which comes naturally to me and in which I have been trained. It may be characterized politely as analytical, or critically as argumentative; and can be applied to practically anything, not only to technical philosophy. I need to apply it to the Christian faith, which I believe has plenty of life in it for future generations.

Much of this book originated in lectures and talks which I have been asked to give over the years. I look back on these agreeable occasions with gratitude to the people who so kindly invited me and entertained me and my husband. Sentences and paragraphs from the lectures have been embedded here and there in this book from the time when I first began to put it together.

Its three-part structure comes from three talks to primary school teachers about my book, *Finding and Following*, in October 1996 at the Kingston Centre, Stafford.

Chapter 1 is based upon the Leveson Lecture which I gave in 2005 at the Leveson Centre, Temple Walsall, Birmingham, on "The Experience of Aging: A Challenge to Christian Belief" (fourth Leveson Lecture, published as Leveson Paper 11). I am grateful for permission to use this material again.

I have also drawn on:

> two lectures in Wells cathedral, in September 1989, on "Visions— Church and Community Looking to the '90s'";

> a lecture at St George's House, Windsor, in January 1999, on "A Philosopher's View of Belief in God in the Twenty-first Century";

> and a lecture in Norwich Cathedral in November 2002, on "Risk and Responsibility," under the kind auspices of Rosslie and Stephen Platten at the Deanery.

I believe that God the Holy Trinity is indeed personal, alive and active, neither abstract Idea nor inert Thing, transcending masculine or feminine gender. So I refrain from using pronouns, "he," "she," or "it," for God, except when I am quoting other people's words or telling other people's opinions.

Helen Oppenheimer
Jersey, Channel Islands, 2013

Part I
Believing

1

Terms of Reference

Som unknown Joys there be
Laid up in Store for me;
To which I shall, when that thin Skin
Is broken, be admitted in.
THOMAS TRAHERNE, "SHADOWS IN THE WATER"

THOMAS TRAHERNE CALLED TO mind what it was like to be a child, by telling how in his "unexperienced Infancy" he was fascinated by the reflections he could see in puddles. He met another world "By walking Men's reversed Feet"; but he could not reach the people he could see down there, upside down in the water. "A Film kept off that stood between." He could imagine earth and heaven as two adjacent but separated worlds, with hope that there might in due course be a way from the one to the other.[1]

If one looks at fish in an aquarium, the same image comes to life. They cannot see out. Looking into the side of the tank at their level, through the water up to the surface, what one sees is an opaque boundary, like a silver ceiling. But people above the fish tank can look down into the water and see the fish swimming about in their everyday world below.[2]

1. This chapter is based upon my Leveson Lecture 2005, at Temple Walsall, Birmingham.

2. I first suggested this image in "The Experience of Aging" in Concilium (1991); and referred to it in my Making Good, 118–19; and in my Leveson Lecture "The Experience of Aging" 2005, 13–14.

We cannot see out of the aquarium of human life, but it appears to be lit from above and some of its contents seem to have arrived from elsewhere. The analogy is not supposed to provide proof that beyond the limits of our sight there is a heaven full of people, where we shall one day be admitted in. What the image offers is not a claim but a disclaimer: a hopeful way of acknowledging our present ignorance, so as not to be defeated by it.

A dead goldfish will float to the surface of the water and somebody will take it away. It will not aspire to be reborn up above in a different environment, breathing our air. The image of human beings inhabiting a fish tank is what used to be called a "conceit," a bright idea which should be life-enhancing and even illuminating, but is not meant to be taken too solemnly. It can suggest to would-be Christians who need encouragement a practical notion of one-way visibility.

Not all Christian believers are as limited in their vision as fish in an aquarium, and some have had experiences of being "caught up to the third heaven,"[3] but most people have in common our ordinary inability to see out. At times when prophecy is muted, when the good news is coming through faintly and it is too easy to believe that this life is all there is, a whimsical image may help to banish despondency.

The disclaimer announced by making a start with swimming fish underlies all the arguments of this book. I do not imagine that I can see out of the fish tank into the world beyond. I have to start more prosaically from where I am and look around from my own particular point of view. Since the inhabitants of our world are far more diverse than fish in a tank, I must not dogmatize about what other people may be able to see, but I can report on what the universe looks like to me. A Christian who has been living in the aquarium and wondering about reality through eight decades need not suppose that she ought to claim some supernatural vision, but she should by now have something to say to commend the faith she does hold. The fish tank provides the terms of reference. The perspective of an argumentative octogenarian is the less fanciful starting point.

How can someone who belongs to the twentieth century and inevitably looks backwards presume to look forwards, and say anything constructive about Christian belief in the twenty-first century? The fatal phrase "When *I* was young" can foster a downhearted frame of mind. The assumptions people make now seem to have changed; the church looks irrelevant, especially on a Sunday morning; intelligent good people are not so much incredulous

3. 2 Cor 12:2–4.

about the Christian faith as ignorant about what they are supposed to believe; the things that mattered in one's youth are discounted . . . How are the children of the millennium going to finish the sentence, "My grandmother used to say . . ."? When I was taken to church as a child, it was a worrying thought that the congregation seemed to consist entirely of elderly ladies. When they had gone, would Christian belief die out? As time went by, I realized that every new generation is aging. Congregations still seem to consist largely of elderly ladies; and now I have become one of them. I have the responsibility to encourage the people following on now and not to put difficulties in their way. Taking stock of my position is not a matter of supposing that I know best. It is a matter of identifying a quantity of data that has gradually accumulated and which needs sorting out to make it more readily available.

Rather than a mathematical proof, QED, of another world beyond, an old Christian should be able to offer an *apologia*, a progress report on the live possibility of faith. While youth is discovering new ideas, age can set about collecting and presenting ideas already given, like the householder who brings out of his treasure things new and old,[4] in this case mostly old. Arranging what one has learnt and offering it to one another is not pointless wool-gathering.

The experience an octogenarian has to offer is likely to be a complex mixture of maturity gained and strength lost. If one thinks of all humanity, this particular starting point has been rare. Most human beings have never been so old. But today more people reach a time when they have not only outlived their parents and grandparents, as was to be expected, but have grown older than their parents and grandparents ever grew. Old age is nowadays a normal enough experience to serve as a introductory case study for pondering whether faith in God is borne out by life.

To begin by describing what human existence looks like, from the viewpoint of someone who has lived for a good while, can be a way of rooting theology in experience, rather than flying off into fantasy. Anyone who wants to commend the Christian faith must look seriously at the character of the world where we have to live. Longevity offers a sample of ordeals and joys, which provide a context for the question whether the universe in which we are placed can possibly be, in fact, an antechamber to heaven. The characteristic blessings and trials of age invite attention to the ordinary ambivalence of human life, which supplies the raw material for any realistic worldview. Can

---

4. Matt 13:52.

we really believe that it was a good Creator who placed us here? Is life too arbitrary, too pointless, indeed too grim, as people actually find it, to have been inaugurated by a good God? Can glory prevail over gloom?

Long before they grow old, human creatures have to come to terms with the passing of time, whether for celebration or regret. The compulsory experience of aging is more than an extra concluding stage. It belongs to human life all along. Aging does not begin at eighty or seventy, nor even at sixty. We have all been growing older as far back as our memories go. We keep on leaving our junior selves behind. Realizing that one is *too* old may start at three, four, five . . . It begins with being told not to be a baby: "You're a big girl now." The little brother is the one on her lap, while the older sister has the alarming adventure of going to school. As people get older the pace quickens and they add year to year rather than month to month: not "five and a half exactly" but "in his fifties."

Human beings have assorted incompatible prejudices about what aging means. Fears of "crabbed age" and doddery feebleness compete with hopes of continuing to grow up towards respected maturity. Some of us, when we consider whether life is good, find it reassuring that the ordinary is as authentic as the ecstatic and the agonizing. If there is indeed a God who made us, God is evidently not too majestic to make room for triviality as well as grandeur.

There are small-scale benefits of aging that are not too insignificant to be counted as valid encouragements, making space for hopefulness lest gloom about our prospects should take over. There comes a time when one is offered a tolerant or even a respectful hand down the steps. It stops being compulsory to regard plunging into cold water as a treat. There are requirements, like wearing fashionable but uncomfortable clothes, which there is no need to try to meet. Better still, it is not one's responsibility to say No to enterprising and argumentative children when really one is on their side.

Experience cannot be counted on to bring wisdom, but it may well bring prudence. One finds out how to recognize in advance some of the toes one might tread on and the foolish mistakes one might make. People who have learnt by trial and error to take more care may find that instead of being more fearful they can be braver. To be gauche is an affliction of immaturity. To grow out of feeling awkwardly juvenile may allow the fun of being a little eccentric.

The experience of aging is less uniform than ever, now that more of us live longer, growing old in variegated ways, both for ill and also for good.

When people grumble about the modern world as if all its changes were for the worse, they should consider modern medicine. Keats died at 26 of tuberculosis. Jane Austen died at 42. Today they could surely have lived longer and left us more of their work. Shakespeare's "old John of Gaunt" could be called "time-honored" in his fifties;[5] and Shakespeare himself died at 52. A good many of our contemporaries have recovered from illnesses that would have killed them a hundred years ago. Modern medical skills have given us a reasonable hope for a sort of slab of good time interposed between middle age and departure. People retire from their jobs but not from satisfying activity.

Getting older can be compared with making mayonnaise. The more oil is already put in, the more stable the emulsion is and the bolder one can be about adding the oil faster. Protecting elderly people from upsetting innovations is too easy a stereotype. Grandparents may allow themselves to be less shockable than the younger ones who are in the thick of the struggle and have to take the responsibility. Young people are sometimes surprisingly conformist in following the current fashions, even when they think they are being rebellious. Old people can risk saying what they really think.

Of course the aged are not to be typecast as tranquil or as lively, any more than they should be typecast as easily upset. It is neither respectful nor kind to foist upon old people the notion that they must all reach "exalted standards of serenity and wisdom."[6] Elders are still individuals, tiresome and splendid in different ways, as much as young people are. To treat them as distinct characters, to take the trouble to find out what they are really like, is one main way to honor them.

There are indeed blessings to be realized and aging people do well to encourage one another to look around them as well as looking back. There is a big But to be faced. Whatever good we find ourselves able to say about getting old must not be unsaid, but it must be balanced by what needs to be said on the other side.

Longevity cannot be relied upon to provide plain evidence that God is good. It would be smug and insensitive to join unthinkingly in singing the praises of the stage of life that is now being called the "third age."[7] The longer people live, the clearer it becomes that the experience of aging is not monochrome. For some people aging does mean maturing; for many

5. Shakespeare, *Richard II*, I, 1, 1.

6. Coleman, "Is Religion the Friend of Aging?," 18.

7. Ibid., 12.

it means becoming more decrepit. Some of us achieve our long-standing goals and some of us realize that there are plenty of happy experiences that we shall never have or never have again.

The passage of time does indeed endow some people with "honor, love, obedience, troops of friends."[8] Some of us are blessed with the awe-inspiring delight of seeing our children's children[9] and even our children's grandchildren. Some, like the Psalmist, "shall bring forth more fruit in their age: and shall be fat and well-liking."[10] *But*, likewise, it is just as ordinary an experience for relentless time to take away the everyday blessings that people could once take for granted and leave them with the prospect of "second childishness and mere oblivion."[11] Our seniors are not there any more and then one by one our friends depart. It is not realistic to expect many octogenarians to go on from strength to strength like Titian, Verdi, or Gladstone.

For all the wonders of modern medicine, it is still true that what doctors can do for their patients is patchy. As people grow older in the twenty-first century there are still plenty of damaging disabilities lying in wait for them. Many people become too frail to go on living in their own familiar homes. Many more are cut off from comfortable sociability by deafness. There are still a large number who lose the sight of their eyes: which happens with special cruelty to scholars who depend on reading. When someone past threescore years and ten has a human lapse of memory, the word "Alzheimer" trips readily off our tongues, perhaps in the hope that we can fight fear better by naming it.

The characteristic hopeful and good aspects of aging seem mostly to belong to the time of life so agreeably commended as the "third age." We have to face the fact that at some time, and, it must be emphasized, at some unpredictable time, the "fourth age" begins. People's lives are suddenly or gradually dismantled; and reorganizing their belongings and their habits is not the positive experience that moving house can be in one's youth. Growing old happens to people in random good and bad ways: gentle for some, traumatic for others. However cheerfully people celebrate their birthdays, most of them would prefer their time to pass more slowly. They certainly do not look forward to becoming really old.

8. Shakespeare, *Macbeth*, V, 3, 23.

9. Ps 128:7.

10. Ps 92:13.

11. Shakespeare, *As You Like It*, II, 7, 163.

One of the hardest things for people who are used to being reasonably effective is becoming a back number. The battles we won or lost in our youth evidently do not matter any more and the comprehension we reached is no longer relevant. The things we learnt the hard way are now of no account. In days gone by, people used to honor their seniors and pity little children. That is reversed now. Children are important people and it is the aged who are pitiable. Respecting the elderly means being polite to them and trying to provide them with comfortable surroundings. It does not mean asking for their advice.

Teilhard de Chardin in *Le Milieu Divin* introduced his Christian optimism by starting with an eloquent acknowledgement of what he called the "diminishments" of human life.[12] In a section forbiddingly called "The passivities of diminishment", he identified "that slow, essential deterioration which we cannot escape: old age little by little robbing us of ourselves and pushing us on towards the end . . . what a formidable passivity," he exclaimed, "is the passage of time . . ."[13] He meant, I take it, the fearful inexorable uncontrollability of time moving on.

It is the arbitrariness, the lack of control, which hits hard. When one reaches the age of outliving one's contemporaries and going to more funerals than weddings one finds oneself helplessly asking Wordsworth's inexorable question, "Who next will drop and disappear?"[14] Robert Browning wrote characteristically, "Grow old along with me: the best is yet to be";[15] but in fact Elizabeth Barrett Browning did not grow old along with her husband.

A major reason for pessimism that is apt to be in the front of people's minds, often nominated as *the* major trouble the prospect of aging brings, is the fear of losing their autonomy. People say, "I don't mind so long as I don't get dependent" and what they mean is only too clear. Helplessness is a dreadful trial, even to the extent of undermining people's humanity; but perhaps some of even this worry may be over-emphasized. Heaven forbid that autonomy should be reckoned as not important; but when it is built up as the one thing that matters, it is time to be counter-suggestible.

There is a balance to correct. A tendency is appearing, in the name of "respect for persons," for autonomy to be so valued as to become an idol.

12. Teilhard de Chardin, *Le Milieu Divin*.

13. Ibid., 60–61.

14. Wordsworth, "Extemporary Effusion Upon the Death of James Hogg," *Poetical Works*, vol. IV, 277.

15. Browning, "'Rabbi Ben Ezra," stanza 1, *Dramatis Personae* in *Poems*, vol. I, 777–81.

In everyday life we are all dependent in all manner of ways, not all of them bad nor even regrettable. Some people bake their own bread or service their own cars, but few of us eat entirely home-grown food or make all our own clothes, and we should not be better and stronger people if we did. The support of other people, known and unknown to us, sets us free to develop whatever particular capacities may be our own.

Dependence is a matter of degree and the extent to which human beings find it irksome is also a matter of degree. For some people, young and old, what they want and need is to be allowed to fend for themselves, to act on their own, to take risks, to have adventures. Their families and friends are bound to worry, but they do their part by not interfering. For other people, freedom is more alarming and letting themselves be molly-coddled is a temptation, not an affliction. Those are the ones who need stirring up to value their autonomy more. Laziness that battens on other people, and can be quite unscrupulous, is unmistakably a *sin*. Let me agree; but let me say, on the other side, that prickly pride, taking its stand on independence, is a sin that is still less endearing. It is more graceful to acknowledge our indebtedness with gratitude than never to incur any indebtedness. When someone's friends and neighbors take real pleasure in being kind, it is best to humor them, to take their arms and walk with them. It is fitting to receive their goodwill gratefully, rather than to rebuff them even in the name of autonomy.

It is a pity to set up a self-defeating competition for the status of helper rather than helped. "She is the sort of woman who lives for others—you can always tell the others by their hunted expression."[16] William Wordsworth learnt a more promising lesson from the old Cumberland beggar, that one way of being good to people is to allow them the pleasure of being generous. The "poorest poor," or we might substitute the "oldest old," can be glad when they find out how they *themselves* can bless and encourage other people, truly doing them a favor by happily appreciating their help. The hand down the steps, or the seat in the bus, convey two-way blessings. The morality that Christians are supposed to have learnt is concerned with *inter*dependence, reciprocity, bearing one another's burdens.

The argument has been weaving about from good to bad and back again; and this is intentional. The point of this "on the one hand"-"on the other hand" argument, this mixture of appreciation and foreboding, is to approach the possibility of faith and the question mark human troubles

16. Quoted by C. S. Lewis's devil Screwtape in *The Screwtape Letters,* Chapter 26.

put against it, by continually keeping hold of truthfulness. To be counter-suggestible may be the most honest stance to take up. Sometimes we should decline to think what we are told to think and refuse to relax in a given point of view. "Yes but" is often an apt response.

Truth demands that we shall not call anything good when we ought to know that it is not. We need not, we *must* not, adopt a relentlessly rosy outlook and pretend that length of life is bound to be splendid, as if anyone who finds it a burden must be ungrateful or faint-hearted. That does not mean that what we need is a compromise, some sort of middle view. It is easy but not much help to say that we find old age to be partly good and partly bad, so that we can be *moderately* content about growing old. That is honest enough; but only by not saying anything in particular.

There is a slogan that is more useful than "either/or" or "half and half"; and that is "both/and." Truth is found, not by denying one set of facts, nor by sitting on the fence, but by setting contraries alongside each other and trying to be fair to each of them. The optimists and the pessimists about old age are both justified. Looking at what our world is like, we have to say that human life is full of hope *and* fear. If optimism is to prevail, this will not happen by people refusing to recognize the fear and saying "Of course it's all for the best," but by people doing something about what makes us afraid.

There is plenty which is being done about the troubles that beset people at different stages of their lives, and plenty more that could be done; and there are many people who indeed are doing it. Indeed one should say "both/and" again about these apparent alternatives, doing or thinking. Human beings are the kind of animal that both thinks and acts. Their thinking itself is something they *do*; and most of them think in order to prepare for doing. Thinking is not usually an academic exercise, separate from action. It has practical results. Taking thought lays the foundations for realistic activity. If people today think justly about growing old, people tomorrow may act wisely and the optimists may realistically hope to prevail over the pessimists. Meanwhile it has to be acknowledged that at present both have reason on their side.

When we really must call aging a struggle, we may hope to find it an exhilarating struggle. We need not leave one another to struggle in isolation. People can set about encouraging each other to find every stage of human life worthwhile, appreciating one another's achievements and honoring their experience, not least if they are fortunate enough to find the Christian story about human life believable.

Rather than either resigning themselves to becoming more and more out of date, or making foolish efforts to be trendy, they can be encouraged by ancient words which link past and future together: "Walk about Zion, and go round about her: and tell the towers thereof"—and the point of the excursion is—"that ye may tell them that come after."[17] People who take heed of past history rather than casually setting it aside will be more careful about demolishing it and may be enabled to build on it more securely. Without presuming to instruct new generations about how to go on from here, they can invite attention to the foundations on which we are standing. The contribution of a theologian, trained as a philosopher, should be to consider, in the light of all the data, what is the truth about the universe and its inhabitants.

17. Ps 48:11–12.

2

Matter and More

And yet, when the Son of Man comes,
will he find faith on earth?

LUKE 18:8

I HAVE ADMITTED HOW BURDENSOME old age can be, which may have been, or at least seemed, regrettably dispiriting. It is fair to keep going back to *both/and* to redress the balance. The experience of aging has more to offer than compensations to make up for what is lost. Old age can hope to find positive blessings and even to make real contributions. Though seniority is no supreme vantage point, it is a significant perspective, a viewpoint indeed, not a place for dumping rubbish.

A Christian who has come this far, having started in an earlier century, indeed an earlier millennium, cannot take for granted either that ancient traditions will last for ever, or that the "good old days" have gone for good. Someone who is disposed to make a stand on Christian faith today can well hope not to meet with dire persecution, but will have to confront the mindset which confidently discards any reality beyond the natural phenomena that people can handle. If the gospel is still where hope is based, it needs to be presented and re-presented. It used to seem obvious that our universe is illuminated from outside, but the onus of proof has shifted. Combative atheists suppose that the battle is all but won.

Is belief in God the unfounded invention of timid people dreading death, who cling to flimsy hopes and tell themselves doggedly that they will surely see their departed loved ones again one day? Skeptics look on faith as an outdated promise of pie in the sky. They readily take it for granted that physics is the whole truth about nature and humanity, underestimating the strength of the ancient ordinary conviction that there are more things in heaven and earth than material objects. But while skeptics accuse believers of basing their supernatural assertions upon baseless assumptions, so likewise are the skeptics open to criticism for their hasty and casual denials.

The godly and ungodly antagonists cannot fight a straightforward old fashioned battle, positive versus negative, because they find nowadays in the space between them a large ill-defined crowd, who prefer what looks like a comfortable compromise. Many people find materialism inadequate, not because they firmly believe the ancient specific Christian doctrines about the nature of God and the coming of God's Son, but because they take seriously their deep-rooted instinct that *matter* is not all there is and that the concept of *spirit* does mean something important.

These contemporaries are offended by militant atheism, but neither are they in sympathy with dogmatic theology. They do not want to be kindly told that really they are Christians all along. Nor do they want their sincere searching to be rejected as defective by self-confident pious conformists. Traditionalist believers may think that such indefinite spirituality is cheating, but they would do better to try to build on it rather than to despise it. More constructively, Christians could remember and take heed of the saying ascribed to the Lord, "he that is not against us is for us."[1]

Open-minded explorers ought to include in their data the experience of reverent awe, which is as characteristically human as far-fetched make-believe. There is evidence, going further back than our branch of humankind, of something like religious practice among *homo sapiens Neanderthalis*. The burial of their dead was apparently not merely hygienic. Yet it was hardly a soothing mystery which impelled a Neanderthal community to make a hole at the base of somebody's skull and then surround that skull with a formal circle of stones.

If that find about 40,000 years old, at S. Felice Circeo on the coast between Rome and Naples, is too primitive to provide any encouragement for rational faith in the twenty-first century, more recent history is relevant. Our ancestors living in the last few centuries were as sophisticated as ourselves. Some of them were congenial, some less so; but when one dips into

---

1. Mark 9:40; Luke 9:50.

their writings[2] one main impression which emerges is a remarkable absence of incredulity. They would die for their God; they would persecute for their God; they would moralize about one another's duty to God; but they did not feel obliged to begin by offering arguments for believing in God at all. It is fair to say that for most of human history religious belief has been, in computer language, the default position. Faith has been reckoned at least as a live option, which human beings have generally taken to be respectable, neither naive nor eccentric.

The argument is not settled, either way. Natural as many human beings find it to believe in God, honest believers have to realize now that their default position appears to have been overridden. The plainest reason why belief in God used to seem so obvious used to be the claim that "design needs a designer." An unbeliever could be challenged to explain how our complex world ever happened, in which such remarkably well-adapted organisms as human beings live and grow and diminish and die, unless there is a Creator who started it off and arranges everything, who can be trusted to know best. Charles Darwin did away with that argument, by showing how living creatures can evolve of their own accord, without needing a Designer. In the twenty-first century, agnosticism and atheism are as intellectually respectable as faith. Yet nor has materialism become obvious. It is not true that reality has been shown to consist only of corporeal objects. Much more can be said truly about human life than can be expressed as physics and chemistry.

Nowadays schoolchildren are taught more about the created world than about the Creator. They should not be too resistant to mind-stretching paradox, since they already find it in their science lessons. If they are learning to be awestruck at how astonishing the phenomena of nature are, they have by no means taken an ungodly turning. On the contrary, they are setting off on a route which leads in a hopeful direction for faith. Heaven forbid that their elders, who have arrived at their traditional creed by traveling along a well-marked path that bypassed physical science, should block the way for learners to find the glory of God in the physical world.

The latest up-to-date road map is informative about the superb scale and complexity of nature, but offers now a route that bypasses the Christian church. Scientists can be encouraged to explore, without theologians being deterred. The God who is Maker of heaven and earth is not obliged to go

---

2. See, for example, Rowell, et al., *Love's Redeeming Work*, an anthology of Anglican Christianity.

through the proper channels, and is surely able to keep in touch with human beings in many ways. It is strange how little notice Christians take of their Lord's teaching that some of the insiders are really outside and that the outsiders are the ones who are finding their way in.[3]

While theologians ponder heavenly data, people whose vocation is to be scientists study and analyze their earthly data. What may bring any of them near to the kingdom of God is not the contents of their syllabus, the material or spiritual subject matter that they find given and try to describe and elucidate, but their willingness to wonder at what they find.

Believers who proclaim the *truth* of the gospel and declare the *goodness* of the Creator should remember that *beauty* too is a value, which lights up nature and animates the words people use for giving an account of the created world. In Psalm 65, the "wonderful things" God shows are dawn and dusk, familiar phenomena that may be explained by physics but are not reducible without remainder to physics. The Psalmist addresses the Almighty as "thou that makest the outgoings of the morning and evening to praise thee." Since the days when that prayer first gave expression to human reverence, natural science has become increasingly mysterious, not plainer and more prosaic.

Readiness to be awestruck may be a first step towards escaping from the skeptical limits drawn by scientific analysis, so as to become aware that describing all the physical processes accurately may actually not be enough for describing everything. The grandeur and the intricacy of the natural world and the particular glory of human language, by which people explore their experience and describe it in words, provide human creatures with glimpses of realities, not mere fancies, which go beyond the limitations of material stuff. *Going beyond* indeed is what "transcendence" means.

Christians may be impatient with such vague and tentative spiritual awareness, setting out on a better signposted and less roundabout route towards recognizing the glory of God, who is Spirit.[4] They should acknowledge on the way that the God whom they have learnt to worship as the Holy Trinity is not the exclusive property of the Christian church, any more than the God of Abraham, Isaac, and Jacob belongs only to the chosen people of Israel. How dare Christians deny that people who have not found traditional piety any help may already, now, have valid experience of spiritual reality, finding themselves in touch with the *Holy Spirit* in person?

3. Matt 25:40.
4. John 4:24.

It is all very well to find and grasp inspiring encouragement, but a Christian who want to inspire and convince other people must keep facing the challenge in the first epistle of Peter, "Always be prepared to make a defense to anyone who calls you to account for the hope that is in you."[5] Disciples should affirm their faith as grand and wonderful indeed, but primarily as true. The gospel is founded upon the statements that Christians make about *facts*. Thinking believers must be ready to marshal the evidence, in order to sustain their own faith and to enable them to commend it.

The argument that relies upon the human phenomenon of religious awareness, as the proof that transcendence is not nonsense, gives a foothold for belief that is somewhat shaky. Feelings of awe help to show that faith is coherent, but they cannot establish for anybody else the real existence of God. Just as for some people piety seems instinctive, for many other people nowadays specific religious conviction seems neither attainable nor desirable. Piety, as doubters see it, looks irresponsible: incurably defective or at best dubious. Bishop Butler wrote to John Wesley that claiming "extraordinary revelations'" is "a very horrid thing."[6] When rational people are invited to commit themselves, they must be shown evidence they can examine, or offered arguments they can follow. The inquirer who demands reasons for Christian hope is not a foe, but is quite likely to be oneself.

A statement of what I believe, an apologia, needs an apologetic, a considered defense.[7] The Christian faith in which I was born and brought up, which I am fortunate enough to find convincing and sustaining, affirms a creed that makes particular characteristic truth-claims, more definitely substantial than suggested moral guidance for human living. The more I hope that the gospel is the truth about the universe, and pledge my loyalty to Jesus Christ the Son who came to reveal God, the more I need to be prepared to defend my faith when challenged,[8] not forgetting the proviso, "yet do it with gentleness and reverence."

In a multi-cultural society, it should be part of children's education to give religious believers a fair hearing and attend to their assertions. It is honest, not muddling, to say something like this: "We agree about some things. We disagree about others. As you grow up you will need to make up

5. 1 Pet 3:15.

6. Bishop Butler, Letter to John Wesley 16 August 1739, in Bulter's *Works*, vol. 2, appendix 3, 435.

7. See above, Chapter 1, page 5.

8. 1 Pet 3:15.

your minds. But ask Christians what Christians believe and Muslims what Muslims believe. And ask people who have no religious faith what they do positively believe." It need not be muddling to tell children, "Most likely none of us has got it completely right yet." That is the sort of idea children can understand, because it is fair and children value fairness.

What is muddling is to say, "There is no true or false about it'" It is unhelpful to sit on the fence and not make it plain that by now one has arrived at some firm opinions. If believers are clear about their own beliefs and respectful about other people's, then they can say politely, "I think you are wrong about that," and try to persuade each other. When they are not sure, they ought to say so.

3

The Argument from Value

Senior devil teaching his nephew how to tempt:
You see the little rift? "Believe this, not because
it is true, but for some other reason." That's the
game.

C. S. Lewis, *The Screwtape Letters* [1]

CHRISTIANS REALIZE THAT MANY of their skeptical contemporaries are as morally serious as they are. At this point a red herring swims into view. Real objective values are indeed something that believers and unbelievers have in common. So now Christians seize upon what seems to be the argument they need for convincing doubters that God is real. How can these values we share hold up, unless there really is a divine Lawgiver who is the Source of morality? If we agree that human laws depend upon properly constituted authority for their validity, where is the authority that makes moral laws valid? Could morality stand on its own, without the authority of a divine Legislator? Believers readily suppose that if there were no God issuing commandments, goodness and badness would have no firm basis and would be merely matters of taste that we would have to decide for ourselves.[2]

---

1. Chapter 23.

2. This chapter is a recapitulation of arguments I first set out in *Making Good*, e.g. Chapter 2, "Goodness"; and passim. See also Oppenheimer (2006) e.g. p.26.

People who already believe in God, and who also have no doubt that moral values are real, put these two certainties together and offer this ethical confidence of theirs as a good reason for any moral person to understand that God does indeed exist. "If you want valid good and evil," they insist, "You must have faith." As they see it, their godless contemporaries are unable to identify objective right or wrong and must manage without any moral principles, except for whatever people happen to choose for themselves as good. No wonder then that when belief is lost values begin to collapse all around us. C. S. Lewis pointed out the trap of trying to make convenient use of God's authority as a means to an end, even a desirable end.[3] But Christians still go on giving the impression that the reason for recommending religion is to uphold morality, because without God our notions of goodness would be merely subjective, so that one moral stance would be as good as another.

How dare we try to make God part of a package deal, good value for humanity because the morality we positively want is available only as included in the whole parcel of doctrine, which we had better therefore accept? It is in order for a tour operator to say, "If you want to go on this holiday you cannot travel on a different plane." It will not do for Christians to say, "If you want values, you must board the plane of faith." It is a mistake to suppose that if we intend our children to grasp the difference between right and wrong, we must teach them religion. That is false to both values and faith.

The distinctive task for people who preach the gospel is not to prop up otherwise wobbly morality, but to witness to the truth about God, which of course includes God's real objective goodness. Christians should not commend their faith mainly as the way to get people to behave better, but because they believe that the Christian account of what God is like and what God has done is true. Its mattering does not make it true; but if we find that it really is true, then we can see how much it matters.

To tell people to worship God, not for God's own sake but as a means to an end, a way of backing up morals, is not only irreverent towards God but is also arrogant towards supposedly immoral unbelievers. Religious people have no right to claim a monopoly of goodness. If they first keep their eyes on truth, then they may gladly cherish the hope that if faith is where they arrive, they will find their morality illuminated and their struggles inspired by God's grace.

3. See heading at beginning of chapter; and Oppenheimer, *Making Good,* 8.

Christian faith is not primarily about ethics, although many people, both believers and unbelievers, seem to think that it ought to be. People in and out of the church are apt to work on the assumption that we need the church to "uphold standards," because it keeps on steadily teaching people, especially children, the difference between right and wrong. The villains are supposed to be the liberals, who are abandoning the standards and encouraging people to do just what they feel like, with chaotic results.

The people who do blur the distinction between right and wrong are not after all the easy-going liberals, who recognize authentic values but are inclined to question whether traditional moral rules must always be obeyed, but the *relativists*, who are not starting from an accepted moral tradition but have to set about making up their own. Responsible liberals, who may well be Christians, are far from jettisoning morality. Their understanding is that right and wrong are complicated and often hard to discover; and that we ought to be less legalistic and more open-minded and generous when we come across unfamiliar ethical ideas. That should by no means commit liberal-minded Christians to the notion that "anything goes."

The belief that people have to choose their values for themselves, because there is no objective right and wrong, is not coming from the liberal wing of the church, but from secular philosophy. It is hardly an exaggeration to call this rather high-minded relativism a kind of orthodoxy in some quarters. If children are being taught that morality is a matter of choice not a matter of fact, or if they are picking relativism up from the world around them, breathing it in as part of the atmosphere, they are being taught something which is indeed contrary to belief in God.

There is work to be done, to see and to show that relativism is not good enough for human beings, that morality after all is a matter of truth and that people can be right or wrong about right and wrong. This is not specially Christian work. Believers and unbelievers could do it together. Real values are part of our equipment as human beings, not reserved for Christians nor even for religious believers.

Liberals, believing or unbelieving, are not enemies of truth. They are people who understand, as a Christian should, that we ought to honor other people and respect their ways of looking for truth. We need to be alert to the likelihood that people may find different important truths from ours. Sometimes we have to say, "I think you are wrong," but we may quite often find ourselves saying, "We're both right," or even, "Perhaps we're both wrong." We shall hardly ever say, "There's no right or wrong about it."

Whether someone tends to look for traditional or radical answers is partly a matter of temperament, and some of us want to be open to either. We can choose our own best routes to truth, but what we cannot choose is what we shall find when we arrive.

Before they blame today's liberals for betraying values, Christians might look upon our present confusions as a natural backlash against a religious attitude that had gone far away from liberalism. It is not so long since it was dinned in to children that sinners were on a straight road to hell, or at least that God will certainly mete out dire punishment to wrongdoers, if not in hell perhaps in purgatory. It is no wonder that the fading of that conviction has made a difference. Of course people behave better if they are more afraid of the consequences of sin: but that is hardly the motivation good people really want to encourage. To think less about celestial retribution makes a good difference: a gain in mercy, and also a gain in sincerity.

Rather than tying morality to divine promises and threats, Christians should be ready to look out for what they have in common with skeptics. It is not illogical for an unbeliever to mind passionately about right and wrong; and indeed many do. Christianity does not teach that values would collapse unless God propped them up. On the contrary, even God could not prop up values if they could not stand up in their own right.

In Plato's Euthyphro dialogue, the question about the basis of ethics is posed.[4] Do values depend upon divine backing? Does God make something good by commanding it, or does God command it because it is already good? To give the priority to God's command is less reverent than it sounds. It would be morally wrong to worship a despot who might issue arbitrary decrees commanding anything whatever, however pointless or wrong his laws seemed to human beings, and thereby nominate values for us to follow. However powerful that Deity might be, people ought to rebel against him, not obey. The basis of ethics must be that good is good, whether there is a Power to enforce it or not.

People who believe in God affirm that there is indeed a divine Power to whom worship is due. God is to be obeyed, not on account of God's power but in response to God's *holiness,* which is transcendent goodness. Believers trust that their holy God supports them and helps them to be good. Agnostics may lack such trust but still care about morality. They could take as ideals Shadrach, Meshach, and Abednego, who were willing

---

4. See Oppenheimer, *Making Good,* 9, n. 10.

to be cast into a burning fiery furnace rather than worship an idol.[5] These were heroes whose moral integrity did not depend upon supernatural assurance. They hoped that their God would come to their rescue, *but if not* they would anyway not serve King Nebuchadnezzar's gods nor worship the golden image that he had set up.

If there can be ethics without divine backing, what has Christian faith to do with morality? The distinctiveness of Christians is not their ability to distinguish good from evil, but their conviction that the physical universe, in which a great number of living beings have evolved, is the work of God who is Spirit. That is a statement about facts, but it cannot to be reduced to a neutral statement about bare physical facts. The premise that in fact creatures have a Maker, who caused them to exist, is certainly not value-free. If the holiness of God the Creator is more than spooky dreadfulness, human notions about goodness, and indeed human moral judgments, are applicable to God. It is relevant, and reverent, to assert that God is morally responsible for what God has made. If God is good, God must care for the well-being of creatures.

I call myself a Christian humanist, because I hold that human well-being matters morally. I agree with skeptical humanists, that the questions we ask about what is good for humanity, or indeed for any conscious creatures there turn out to be, are questions about how these creatures can flourish: whether they are human beings, fish in an aquarium, wild or domestic animals, inhabitants of outer space, or angels in heaven.[6] Pious people are inclined to identify "humanism" with selfish worldliness. They say, "Down with sinful humanity," rather than, "Up with human beings." They could afford to be more boldly humanist, more concerned about human well-being, without being less Christian. They could be humanists in God's name, valuing the humanity that God has been pleased to make and to redeem. Human creatures should not be deprecated as vermin whose flourishing does not matter, nor devalued as slaves whose only worth is their obedient service.

God's good purpose for a living being is more positive than law making and law keeping, "Thou shalt do this," and "Thou shalt not do that." Rather, the question of what is good for a creature is a matter of what that creature is like: believers will say, how that creature is made. Human beings have evolved far enough to consider their own existence and to ask

---

5. Dan 3:16–18. Lord Lindsay, Master of Balliol, made a lasting impression when he preached on *but if not* to schoolgirls during the war.

6. Cf. Oppenheimer, *Making Good*, 12.

what makes people flourish. They have some understanding of what is worthwhile. Many of them believe that the God who gave them life has provided them with laws to show them how to live well: not a religious definition of "goodness" to get morality started, but practical rules for human flourishing.

To agree that what is good for one creature may be different from what is good for another is by no means to say that goodness after all is "only relative."[7] Variegated goodness is as real and objective as monochrome goodness. A creature cannot decide for itself what will be conducive to its flourishing. The best answer is something that this individual needs to discover, a matter of fact that may turn out to be complex and subtle. I am not entitled to suppose that because I enjoy chocolate, and because I am free to make eating it part of my chosen lifestyle, I can decide that chocolate shall really be good for me. My chocolate-choosing lifestyle may not be a promising way for me to flourish.

To complicate matters further, perhaps what really is good for the creature I am may be to make moral choices and even to be a law unto myself. Sometimes what is objectively right, right as a matter of fact not only opinion, is to follow one's own vocation and allow oneself to be more rebellious or more creative. Humble obedience to tyrannical laws, or conventional conformity to the rules of society, are not promising ways for most people to flourish. So the moral balance may need correcting in favor of autonomous choice rather than rule-keeping, but still without making morality "only relative."

As a straightforward illustration of free choice yielding objective value, I can take *pairbonding* as an example of a way of life which is experienced as actually good for human beings, as it is for various other species such as geese. Faithfulness to one mate is a hopeful way for someone to flourish, because it accords with is what human beings are like, their created nature. From this premise, true statements follow about how they should behave to one another. It does not follow that this way of life must be a given rule for every kind of creature, or even best for every single one of us.

Christians and skeptics may therefore have more in common than they expected. Skeptics about God can still be confident that right and wrong are for discovering, not inventing. They may still very likely find themselves in disagreement with Christians about what behavior will turn out to be right or wrong in practice. Whether this life is the whole story

7. Ibid., 12–13.

makes a difference to what is good for us in our lives now. Believers in God consider the prospect of life beyond death.[8] People who find the Christian story about human existence believable can afford to put less emphasis on short-term happiness, because they believe that their Creator made them for eternal flourishing; but this difference about the facts does not give believers any moral superiority to skeptics.

8. Cf. ibid., 13.

4

Recalcitrant Reality

Look upon the covenant: for all the earth
is full of darkness, and cruel habitations.

PSALM 74:21

STRANGE AS IT MAY seem, it may not always be appropriate for everyone who finds the Christian story believable and sustaining to follow St. Paul's advice to Timothy and preach the word in season and out of
season.[1] Some people's confident faith, which they feel everyone ought to
share, can even make it harder for other people to accept their assurance
that in charge of everything there is a loving God. "It's all very well for
them." If Christians who have grown old in God's service insist relentlessly
that whatever happens everyone must keep thanking God our Creator for
the blessings of our lives, their piety can appear as no help to anyone else
but as a positive hindrance, smoothing over what everyday experience is
like and separating religious people from their fellow human beings.

The troubles of the world stand as a huge objection to an optimistic
outlook.[2] One ordinary example of the ancient problem of evil is indeed
the fact that even such a traditional blessing as long life is found by many
people achieving it to be no blessing at all. "I don't want to go on and on if

---

1. 2 Tim 4:2.

2. Returning here to the problem of evil, the main objection which a responsible
Christian faith has to face, I am drawing upon my Leveson Lecture again, "The Experience of Aging." See also Oppenheimer, *Making Good*, e.g., 16–18, 23, and passim.

that is what it is going to be like." The burdensome vulnerability of bodily existence cannot be ignored for ever.

For unbelievers, the troubles of creation, including the troubles of aging and mortality, are practical, desperately practical; but they are not required also to provide theoretical answers. If there is no God and the universe is not on our side, there is no reason to expect heavenly comfort to be provided for us and we shall just have to do the best we can. It is people who believe in a good God who have to face the huge moral question about why God's creatures should be made to suffer so. If Christians turn away from painful truth and seem not to care, still reiterating that the news is good, they stand convicted of insensitivity. Unless they can somehow justify the ways of God to man, their faith will go by default.

In the face of an intractable problem, it is natural for human beings to look for someone to blame. Once, religious people assumed that the answer to the problem of evil was simple: we must blame ourselves. All our woes are the result of the disobedience of Eve and Adam, so therefore bad fortune must be humbly accepted as the punishment which the sinful human race deserves. If that fruit had never been eaten, we could all have grown old gracefully, or perhaps stayed happily in our prime for ever.

That simple explanation has become incredible. Christians generally understand well now that the universe had a long history before humanity arrived. Many sentient creatures lived on earth before any of them were people who could make moral choices deserving punishment or reward. If the first human beings in their arrogant freedom did all the damage, it would follow that when the dinosaurs preyed upon each other they caused one another no pain. We cannot and should not be satisfied with the notion that all life's victims must have brought their afflictions upon themselves. The Book of Job is the biblical witness that innocent suffering is an authentic problem. The question, "What have I done to deserve this?" is a fair question which often has no plain answer.

Honest people justifiably reject the idea that their troubles are all their own fault. They might more plausibly blame God for the way life on earth is set up. But they are not allowed to blame God; so they stop believing that there is any God in charge. Since Darwin destroyed the argument that there must be a God, because the complex multiplicity of creatures could never have arisen of its own accord without a Designer, many people can and do solve the problem of evil by shedding their faith.

Since I hold on to Christian belief in a good Creator, I am bound to look for a Christian answer to the challenge. If I could not arrive at some sort of hopeful account of the troubles that beset people, I would have no right to go on calling myself a Christian. But if I am satisfied too quickly with a glib answer, I shall have no right to call myself a thoughtful human being. Christians cannot expect to find rabbits in their hats.

There is indeed more to say than, "Cheer up: it's all marvelous really," or even, "It is not for us to question God's inscrutable will." But any attempt to find out what a Christian can say must proceed by way of entering into the problem and properly acknowledging the integrity of the people who are defeated by it. It is far from Christian charity to say *only* "You must have faith". When the Lord's disciples appeal to his saying "Only believe,"[3] they should put it in its context. He had already given his followers good reason for trusting him. He had inspired them with his teaching. He had done marvelous works and was about to do another. The faith that he was asking of them was not blind faith.

Nor was it a moralistic faith caring nothing for human troubles but only for their virtue. When it is stated that Jesus "went about doing good," the plain meaning is that he attended to people's bodily infirmities then and there, even on the Sabbath day, not that he kept preaching to them about their souls. If Christians had a firmer grasp of their hope that somehow at last God's creation shall be recognizably a world full of happiness, uncommitted people would be more likely to realize that they are being offered something they might actually want.

If Christians could understand, and show that they understand, that the problem of suffering is not marginal and that concern about life-diminishing troubles it is not disloyal, they could repudiate the false response to their problems that human happiness does not really matter in God's eyes. To want this life to be worthwhile is not just part of our sinful greed. Christians can be humanist enough to affirm, without heresy, that God's purpose for humanity cannot be limited to dutiful obedience and that there must be more to the meaning of life than keeping moral rules. To tackle the problem of evil we have to go a longer way round, truly entering into the concerns of people who do not take the consolations of faith for granted.

If as a believer I want to convince anyone else that one day right is going to prevail and God's will is going to be done, I must start by honoring the courage of my contemporaries who have to be brave without a God

---

3. E.g., Mark 5:36.

to put everything right in the end. When it turns out that people agree with me in shared values, even when we differ about what we expect will happen, let me not drive a wedge between us, especially not in the name of religion. Since I respect the integrity of unbelievers, I may hope that they will accept my integrity, when I try to explain to them what I believe and why I believe it.

Before I can expect my convictions to carry any weight, I must take heed how far we are already of one mind. People with and without faith can understand one another better, not by arguing and demanding concessions, but by starting with how much we have in common all along, hoping in due course to build on it. There are, as it were, interim ideas that believers can ponder along with unbelievers for encouragement and comfort. Much of what can be said about the predicaments and opportunities of living and aging should be acceptable at least to agnostics.

A secular funeral may set a good example of how honesty can be more encouraging than trite comfort. Christians could recognize, with appreciation, that some people without religious faith come to terms with mortality by unselfishly acknowledging that life goes on and that one generation makes way for another. If people cannot have permanence, they can still look for a kind of fulfilment when they see worthwhile patterns developing from what has gone before.

There is human consolation in noticing how one sometimes feels an honorable kind of relief when a beloved person has died after a long time of going downhill. The expected has happened; and now we can call to mind the lively companion of past days and happy times, without being confronted only by the figure of the reduced human being we knew recently. The familiar person can be recollected in a way that had been blocked. Christians can enter into this encouragement. They can move on from it, to shed light on their belief that the stages of a whole life really are to be gathered up, not only in the mind's eye but in the reality of heaven.

People of faith ought to offer that hope gently not brashly. They ought not to claim to offer a quick and easy route out of the hardships of our world into another better one. Since the Christian hope depends upon a God who came to our rescue without taking short cuts, believers must expect for the present to travel in the same fragile boat as unbelievers. They can learn together how best to cope now with the frightening roughness of the sea, without supposing that the only people who can navigate hopefully are the ones who are fortunate enough to have firm confidence about their destination.

Especially we all need courage. Neither Christians nor skeptics can claim a monopoly of bravery. The cardinal virtue of fortitude was first a pagan virtue and is no less a Christian virtue for that. Fear is a besetting challenge which spoils human happiness, from which believers are not exempt. If they thought they could be safe from such weakness, that would indicate a failure to understand. To be threatened by doubtful dangers is itself an important kind of human suffering that needs to be acknowledged and overcome, not discounted.

Christians are surprisingly apt to forget how important in the teaching of Christ is the commandment not to be anxious.[4] It is noticeably more prominent than the emphasis on chastity that Christian moralists have been so inclined to put first. C. S. Lewis had a practical suggestion, that anxiety may itself be the particular affliction we have to undergo and must take in hand.[5] Often the immediate distress to be borne is uncertainty. To let worries take over is a temptation to be identified and faced. We might anyway come to understand that the virtue of courage does not require comprehensive resignation to every possible ill, as if they were all going to come true together. I am not expected to feel contented in advance about being arthritic *and* blind *and* deaf *and* impoverished *and* all alone. Whatever consolations and compensations there may turn out to be cannot appear until a specific threat has actually materialized.

Dismal and dire things happen: but often not the ones that people have dreaded. It is said that the mustard manufacturers make a living from all the mustard that is never destined to be eaten but is left on people's plates. Likewise we may imagine the devil making a living from all the worries to which people help themselves. The Duc de Saint Simon commented in the early eighteenth century: "For want of other comfort I lived on my courage, telling myself that we seldom experience all the good or all the evil that there is reason to expect."[6] A great deal of worry is wasted. To try to cope faithfully now with imagined ills is counter-productive, like trying to swat a swarm of midges.

From childhood to old age, human beings find satisfaction in shaping good and bad experience into stories; and Christians can be glad to enter into this encouragement. Telling the tale of what has brought people to where they are now allows them to fit it all into their life histories, whether to mourn or to celebrate.

4. E.g., Matt 6:25–34.
5. Lewis, *The Screwtape Letters*, Chapter 6.
6. Saint Simon, *Historical Memoirs*, vol. II, 128.

> With weeping and with laughter
> Still is the story told,
> How well Horatius kept the bridge,
> In the brave days of old.[7]

Shakespeare's veteran of Agincourt will show his scars and

> remember, with advantages,
> The deeds he did that day . . .[8]

The generations are bound together by recollections, re-collections indeed, of small occasions, little rituals, childish jokes, particular traditions. Anyone who has happy memories from youth of beloved older people may have gained more than agreeable entertainment at the time. Once we ourselves are old, we have to beware of entering into what has been agreeably called our "anecdotage"; but many elders have opportunities to offer younger people some idea of what it was like to grow up in our time, why we see some things differently because of the experiences we have lived through. Rationing may have made us obsessive about waste, or the wartime discipline that had to be imposed upon the young people we used to be may have spoilt our tolerance of juvenile disorder. Sometimes we can recount how things have improved. My grandmother planted somewhat feminist seeds in my mind by telling me how uncomfortable it was to wear an obligatory hobble skirt.

There are narratives that can gather someone's life into a whole, arranging maturity and decline in coherent patterns. Some people, like Tennyson's Ulysses, can treat old age itself as a journey of exploration:

> Death closes all: but something near the end,
> Some work of noble note, may yet be done . . .

For the aged Ulysses, the siege of Troy is already long ago, but the poem draws past and future together into one story:

> It may be we shall touch the happy isles
> And see the great Achilles, whom we knew.[9]

Time and retelling can give shape to our experiences when we look back upon them. Some of us remember our school days, not I hope as the

---

7. Macaulay, "Horatius," in *Works,* vol. VIII, 484.

8. Shakespeare, *Henry V,* IV, iii, 51.

9. Tennyson, "Ulysses," lines 51–52 and 62–63, in his *Poems.*

happiest time of our lives, but as a big adventure. Some things that made us downhearted at the time we would not now wish otherwise, when they have become part of a larger whole. Even a tragic story may turn out to have hope in it, if it can eventually be understood as some kind of triumph. That is part of an explanation of how tragedy is a life-enhancing art form.

A world in which evil has been conquered may eventually be more satisfying than a world where everything has always been straightforward.[10] This is no masochistic assurance that suffering is best because pain is "deeper" than joy. Happiness is best: but the best happiness includes elements that would be missing in a world where happiness could be taken for granted. There are valuable crops that the garden of Eden is too sunny to grow.[11] Just as a great human work of art has some sort of intensity, so the real world would be a poorer thing if it were less demanding. A permanently bright existence in which light-heartedness always came easily and happiness was never hard-won, a disengaged and trivial life with no risks, no struggles, no hint of tragedy, would be two-dimensional, even impoverished. The best outcome is neither failure nor easy success, but victory.

When human life is harsh, describing differently what is going on may be a help and it may be the best we can manage; but people who are in too much hurry to tell the tale in their way will carry no conviction. The fact that God's "very good"[12] creation is full of pain is too serious to be set right by creative storytelling. It is no comfort to unhappy people to be told that tragedy is more profound than comedy. The aesthetic judgement, that these troubles are justified by being artistically right, looks even more insensitive than the moral judgment, "We sinners are getting what we deserve."

The suffering of creatures is a formidable objection to faith, which makes inventive ingenuity look simply unfeeling. The accusation, that whatever Power made this world must be heartless rather than good, needs a reply which is not just inspiring but true.[13] If the universe was made for a purpose, its meaning must be findable, not only in the work of imagination, but in real happenings of history.

Christians have a particular account to give of God's dealings with the creation, which they offer, not as an illuminating interpretation to be relished, but as facts to be believed. They tell the story of the Son of God,

---

10. See Oppenheimer, *Making Good*, e.g., 121.

11. See Edwin Muir's poem "One Foot in Eden," Muir, *Collected Poems*.

12. Gen 1:31.

13. See above, Chapter 2, 17.

who has taken the responsibility, paid the price and won the victory: They are prepared to make a defense to anyone who calls them to account for the hope that is in them,[14] calling upon witnesses to back them up, that in the end the complete history of the universe will not turn out to be a crushing tragedy after all, but indeed a Divine Comedy.

14. 1 Pet 3:15.

5

The Project of Creation

Thou dost preserve the stars from wrong:
And the most ancient heavens, through Thee,
are fresh and strong

WILLIAM WORDSWORTH, "ODE TO DUTY"

BEFORE SKEPTICS CAN BE exhorted to put their trust in God, they have the right, and even the duty, to ask fiercely how good people can believe in a God who has made this universe, in which so many innocent people and animals suffer so much. Their doubts cannot be ruled out as presumptuous. Human beings cannot judge God; but in a way they must, because to *worship* God has to be a moral choice. God's holiness cannot be so different from human goodness that ethical notions about responsibility[1] that apply to human actions would fail to apply to their Creator. Some Christians are obliged to heed the skeptical question about how God could be justified in creating such a risky world. No thunderbolt fell upon Abraham for arguing about justice with the Almighty: "Far be that from thee! Shall not the Judge of all the earth do right?"[2] The charge demanding an answer is that whatever Power made this universe cannot be loving at all, but a reckless and brutal demon.

A simple reply is that God sends us adversity in order to educate us in virtue and test our progress; but believers should not be quickly satisfied

---

1. See Oppenheimer, *On Being Someone*, Chapter 17, especially 182, 185, 188f.

2. Gen 18:25.

with the image of a well-organized school exam that may be hard but will assuredly be fair. The real ordeals that human beings face are not so manageable and are often blatantly unfair. Experience provides only too much evidence against faith in a benevolent Deity.

There is more encouragement in the parable of the landowner who sowed good seed in his field but found tares coming up among the wheat.[3] He does not soothingly announce, "It is better so" or "These things are sent to try us." He declares, "An enemy has done this." Something has gone wrong. It is stubbornly part of Christian terms of reference that nature is open to risk. The workings of inanimate nature are surely governed more by impersonal chance than by purposeful providence. Rather than insisting doggedly that everything that happens must have been part of God's good purpose all along, believers are allowed to think of creation as a great enterprise that is not yet complete, which is complex enough to include problems and struggles.

Twenty-first century people are more inclined to ascribe their troubles to random bad luck than to blame a devilish enemy, with or without horns and a tail. What the parable of the tares offers is a realistic acceptance that in a world more solid than make-believe troubles are possible and even likely, and do not have to be called good. The problem of evil would defeat me, if faith meant blindly trusting the inscrutable righteous Author of every happening in this tough universe, who has planned it in full detail, troubles and all, who left nothing to chance, who brooks no criticism because everything is in good order as it is. The creation of a universe that is real, grander than a toy to entertain its Maker, includes the possibility of fearful setbacks.

The question whether creation is worthwhile turns upon whether its inhabitants will be able to understand the whole story at last and be heartily grateful to their Maker. The universe is not untroubled, but is going to be worth the trouble. The—literally—crucial point is that the trouble is God's trouble. Christian belief in God the Creator who "saw that it was good"[4] incorporates belief in God the Deliverer who foresaw the dangers, who joins in the struggle, who bore the cost, who will make it good. Christian faith is based, even more directly than Jewish faith, upon a narrative about what God has done within the history of the world God made.

The God of the old covenant rescued his chosen people from the oppression that had befallen them in Egypt. The God of the new covenant

3. Matt 13:28.

4. Gen 1:31.

rescues all humanity from their sins that have spoilt the harmony of creation, by paying the price on their behalf. So far, so good. Of course Atonement is the heart of the gospel. Sinners who are burdened by the weight of the wrongs they have done receive the good news that Jesus Christ has taken away their sin, has paid the death penalty for them and has defeated death by rising again. Heaven forbid that the gospel of God's mercy should be watered down by sophisticated liberals who fail to take depravity seriously, who suppose that penitence is sick masochism and that easy-going tolerance is the most important virtue.

But to preach God's generous forgiveness for human sin as the complete answer would be to proclaim the Christian hope without grasping the scale of the problem of evil. There is evidently much more wrong with the world than human sins.[5] The argument is valid but incomplete, that pain happens because the creation of people who will excellently do God's will implies the real possibility that they may choose instead to do evil. The "free will defense" of God's goodness, that our sufferings are just and appropriate, since we freely chose to disobey and brought our troubles on ourselves, is only a partial answer to the charge that the Creator is not moral. Because our lives include evils that are not our fault as well as sins that are, the "free will defense" needs to be expanded by spelling out a more comprehensive argument, a "free-standing defense"[6] which looks more carefully at the implications of creating a world.

If people have indeed come into being as small-scale images of God their Maker,[7] then the familiar creativeness of humanity, which we can see at work producing real artifacts, should illuminate what divine creation may be like. We can consider how the conditions of human making might apply by analogy to the work of their Creator. First the contrast must be acknowledged. Divine creation is "from nothing": God needs no raw materials. Then we may affirm the comparison. Though human beings cannot make anything "from nothing," they are not limited to moving existing objects around. Their making is an image of divine creation when they so transform the given raw material that something positively new is brought into being, something more than the sum of its parts.

---

5. See above, Chapter 4, 27.

6. I developed this argument in Oppenheimer, *Making Good*. John Polkinghorne makes a similar point, calling it the "free-process defense," in *Science and Providence*, 5 and Chapter 5.

7. Gen 1:27.

Then, when the work is done, its maker has to have the confidence to relinquish control. Part of the meaning of creation, divine or human, is "letting be." An artifact that is real, not imaginary, is endowed with a certain independence to take its own place as a fact in the history of the world. Books are written to be published. Sculpture is shaped for standing in a public place, not for keeping in a studio. Music, and still more drama, is realized by performance. Cakes are made to be eaten, clothes to be worn, tools to be wielded. Buildings are for inhabiting; and people live in solid houses which stand up without day-to-day alterations. Likewise God's handiwork is freestanding. The word of God the Creator is "Let there be . . ." The more real the creation, the more its maker stops controlling it and lets it exist.

The Creator of the universe has made not only inert things that exist passively, but conscious people who live and grow and exercise choices. For their activity to be real, the physical environment in which they are set does itself need to be inert and passive, reliably continuing in its own way without supernatural tinkering. Predictable providential control would make human life a charade. It is therefore a promising notion, fearful but necessary, that the course of events may go wrong; and that the limits of possible adversity that have to be allowed, on the way to achieving a worthwhile universe, cannot be established in advance, so much and no more.

As soon as one sets about imagining the physics of a world where nothing is permitted to go too badly amiss, one is thinking about producing a puppet show not creating a universe. May a badly built house collapse in an earthquake, but not a whole city? Would a good God let me break my arm, but not my neck? May an adult die, but not a child? May a child die, but not in pain? The idea that history is open to events that are actually contrary to God's will, real evils that are not to be denied or ignored but need to be overcome, is an encouraging thought, because it makes room for the process of creation to be as painful in the meantime as people often find it to be.

Believers in a good Creator are committed to two basic assertions. First, that for the universe to be more real than an entertaining slide-show, its Maker must *let go* in order to *let be*. Second, that for the universe after all to be counted "very good" at last, the Creator who brought it into existence must be *responsible for the cost* of bringing it eventually to fulfilment. The Christian gospel describes what that responsibility meant.

A third essential affirmation is more mysterious. Positive hope that at last there will be a final fulfilment, a permanent completed masterpiece, is indispensable. It is only too easy to establish the need to make room for suffering in the process of creating a real universe, but faith in a good God also requires the actual emergence of an eventual upshot, different from this world-in-the-making but arising out of it, a stable heaven where problems will have been solved, troubles will be over, evil will have been conquered and blessings woven into a whole. Peter Abelard wrapped this hope in Latin poetry:

> Illic ex sabbato succedit sabbatum,
> Perpes laetitia sabbatizantium . . .

> There, now that sabbath-day follows on sabbath-day,
> With joy perpetual keeping the festival . . .[8]

Someone who presents a promising view of the world can be asked for convincing reasons for believing it. The strongest evidence in favor of Christian faith in a Creator and Savior is the experience to which the first Christians bore witness. The God of their tradition still did mighty acts, not only in the legendary past but in the prosaically historical time of the Roman Empire. The life, the death, and the resurrection of Jesus of Nazareth were the data that led his followers to recognize this one particular human being as the revelation of God in person, entering into the history of the world, not imaginary but accessible. Christians accept the good news that God the Creator is securely in charge of the universe, because they found evidence for believing that "God was in Christ reconciling the world to himself."[9]

The Maker of everything was made known as the Redeemer, the cost-payer, who has not stayed safe in heaven, happily aloof. The Creator became human and knows the harm of evil at first hand, taking the responsibility for having set human beings in such a dangerous world. Even more basic than paying the debts of sin, divine atonement means that God endured, in a vulnerable human body, the hurt which God has allowed sensitive creatures to suffer. The Creator values the lives of people enough to bear comprehensively alongside them the cost of permitted evil, including the unyielding toughness of physical reality, as well as the ways human beings hurt and damage one another by the sins that they themselves commit.

---

8. Peter Abelard (1079–1142), "O quanta qualia," *The Oxford Hymn Book*, no. 349 (translation by present author).

9. 2 Cor 5:19.

To affirm that God is *good* applies moral law to the Almighty, declaring that the Judge of all the earth has indeed done right.[10] Dare one paraphrase "God's responsibility" as "God's duty"? Christians call God "Father"; and what they mean by this allows them to recognize that parents have obligations to the children they have brought into the world. Parental love can generally be trusted to transcend the bare demands of law and make duty look irrelevant, but the idea of what they *ought* to do makes sense, especially if doubt is being cast on whether they have done it.

Children generally take their parents' kindness for granted, without putting them under judgment. It would be shocking if they acknowledged their goodness by saying, "Quite right too," or even, "Yes, they were up to standard." But if some captious critic tries to introduce distrust, then the children's secure confidence needs moral defense. Because the problem of evil impugns the justice of the heavenly Father, human creatures must be prepared to back up their assertion that their God has met the responsibility of creation. Christians need to affirm that "God was in Christ,"[11] before they can carelessly relax in the grateful confidence that all is well.

10. See note 2 above.
11. See note 9 above.

6

Question of Fact

Glendower: I can call spirits from the vasty deep.
Hotspur: Why, so can I, and so can any man;
But will they come, when you do call for them?
WILLIAM SHAKESPEARE, *HENRY IV, PART I*, ACT 3, SCENE 3

THE CHRISTIAN HOPE IS based on the biblical accounts of God's actions in human history. If the stories are not true, the hope is ungrounded. "This is the story which inspires me" is not enough, unless I can offer it responsibly as connected with reality. An apologia, an account of where I stand, is all very well, but when I present my faith in God as a live option for convincing enquirers, I cannot do without the backing of an *apologetic*, a defense of the position I am taking.[1]

This is an exacting challenge. To speak about truth is to invite contradiction. As long as people with and without religious belief are contented to cooperate in upholding and commending shared values of Goodness and Beauty, they can be glad to recognize how much they really agree and not fret about how much they differ. There is scope for the idea that everybody is right really, or at least that everybody's opinion is worth hearing. But for faith to be a matter of Truth, more is required than an invitation to adopt a particular set of values as a promising way to live. The truth about the universe is a matter of inexorable fact. People who profess a religious faith are called *believers*. They make statements about what God and the world

1. See above, Chapter 1, 5, Chapter 2, 17.

are like. Their creeds are supposed to tell truly what is the case, and might therefore turn out to be false. Sometimes believers have to contradict things that other people say, because truth matters.

Christian faith is obstinately concerned with facts. Christians have to take sides, refusing to accept the idea that it does not matter whether people of goodwill identify themselves with any religion or none, as if which faith is the best were only a question of opinion after all, to be decided by what people happen to find helpful to them. Of course, we may never know what the truth is. Suppose atheism is true. Christians will never find this out, because we are all going to die, and once we are dead we shall never have to admit to skeptics, "How right you were." Like many believers in various faiths, I am convinced that one day, after death, believers and skeptics will all realize with joy what the truth is: what the facts are. I am expecting, and hoping, to learn that Christianity is the faith that is the nearest to the truth. Some people will find this too hesitant; others will find it not hesitant enough, too dogmatic.

A Christians can make claims about what is true, without claiming any monopoly in virtue for people who accept these claims as valid. I cannot write off as immoral the skeptics who disbelieve the Christian gospel, and I could hardly believe in a God who would write them off, nor even in a God who would receive them grudgingly, saying coldly, "Their unbelief is excused, because they are invincibly ignorant."

When Christians try to make judgments about other people's status in God's eyes, as Peter asked about John, "Lord, what about this man?" they generally get the answer Peter received, "What is that to you? Follow me!"[2] A disciple may persist, "Lord, these doubters matter to me," finding encouragement to argue with the Almighty, both in the Hebrew scriptures and in the Gospels.[3] The divine reply may be anticipated: "They matter infinitely more to me."

Christians must take to heart that their God cares as much about all the unattached uninstructed people "who do not know their right hand from their left"[4] as about the well-brought-up church members and the strenuous converts. The Lord evidently did not set up barriers to keep out nonconformist hangers-on. On the contrary, he particularly welcomed the unqualified outsiders into his kingdom. Whatever "justification by faith"

2. John 21:20–22.

3. E.g., Gen 18:23–33; Mark 7:25–30; and see chapter 5, 34 above.

4. Jonah 4:11.

means, it cannot mean that holding correct theological views is the one necessary condition for being acceptable to Christ.

On the one hand, Christians should be most reluctant to reject other people from their company for failing to believe the right doctrines. On the other hand, they must persist in affirming that there are right doctrines, true statements about God, whether or not human beings have understood them aright. The truth of the gospel concerns facts that might be ascertained. The Bible provides not only inspiration but information.

Any statement that purports to tell the truth about reality must run the risk of being shown to be untrue. Thoughtful Christians cannot hastily abandon the cautious frame of mind that prevailed in twentieth century "theory of knowledge,"[5] which inquired how claims to possess knowledge or to hold valid beliefs can actually be justified. It was dinned into students of philosophy that a statement that purports to be about facts cannot even make sense, let alone be affirmed as true, unless it says something that somebody could find out. One must see what it would mean for it to be tested, and therefore recognize the risk of its being falsified. A sentence is meaningless if, whatever happens, nothing will be allowed to count against it. People who have been informed that London is a great city can travel there and find a real place, which may be different from what they expected. If Christians talk about heaven, they must mean that people can go there one day and see what it is like. If they talk about the vision of God, God must in some sense be visible.

Thoughtful and loyal Christians are sometimes so concerned not to risk talking nonsense that they stop demanding plain assertions or denials. They give up insisting plainly that the creed that they affirm is about matters of fact. Instead of pressing the question "Is this literally true?" these Christian scholars have wise and subtle things to say about different kinds of truth, about myth, poetry and symbolism. Radicals are not apostates. It is the strength of their faith that allows them to take the Christian gospel for granted. But what grounds this strong faith? What persuades them to become and remain believers? At any moment Hans Andersen's small child may call out tactlessly that the Emperor has no clothes on.

A particularly slippery word is "story." Far be it from me to denigrate what is called "narrative theology," or ignorantly to write off current New Testament studies, from which I need to learn much more. But biblical

---

5. See, e.g., Russell, *The Problems of Philosophy*; Broad, *The Mind and Its Place in Nature*; and Price, *Belief.*

scholars who concentrate on how works of literature are developed should be mindful of the risk of letting themselves lose touch with solid facts, slipping from stories to fables, and so to fibs: "Don't tell stories." We comfort frightened children by saying, "Don't cry: it's *only* a story" and leave that thought with them as their equipment for discerning the truth or falsity of the gospel.[6]

When it is recounted that the Lord Jesus gave such and such teaching, or healed such and such a sufferer, or—especially—rose from the dead, something must have happened in those days, or not happened. We may not know and we may have no way of finding out, or anyway not in this life, but we should make it clear that eventually factual questions demand yes-or-no answers. This does not forbid us, rather it obliges us, often to speak tentatively or approximately: "That is probably what happened." "That is one way of expressing what we mean, which still leaves it mysterious."

We are not required always to be literal. Real facts may be best described in figures of speech: "My love's like a red, red rose."[7] Provided the simile succeeds in expressing her recognizable quality, the poetry can be as truthful as prose. It is fact rather than fancy that she is beautiful. She evidently has a vivid personality, but may turn out to be a bit prickly. Someone who said "My love is like a lily" would be describing a different woman, remarkably pure and calm.

Truth can be told by recounting a story that is "ben trovato," true to life rather than true to history.[8] Dr. Spooner never said all the Spoonerisms that are ascribed to him. He may not have asked whether the bean was dizzy; but the stories about him build up an authentic picture of a real individual donnish personality. By all means let us take some of the Gospel stories in this way, not as verbatim accounts of what Jesus said, but as good examples of what he was like, the memories he left.

We may not know for certain whether Jesus did this or that mighty work, but we can know what impression he made, what people could believe about him. Someone who is said to have turned water into wine[9] can hardly have wanted his followers to be life-denying ascetics. Evidently he could be fierce as well as meek and mild. He cannot have been priggish, sanctimonious, or boring. Liberal Christians who are not fundamentalists

---

6. Oppenheimer, *Helping Children Find God*, 3–4.

7. Robert Burns, "O My Luve's Like a Red, Red Rose."

8. Oppenheimer, *On Being Someone*, 168.

9. John 2:1–11.

may fairly encourage one another with sayings like, "My yoke is easy and my burden light,"[10] or "The Sabbath was made for man,"[11] without always stopping first to spell out "We are told that he said this": *on condition* that they do not ignore the reported hard sayings that must have been just as characteristic.

It would be useful if Christians arguing with skeptics about gospel truth would clarify the different ways in which stories may or may not claim to be true. The New Testament accounts should not be called *myths,* if a myth is an illuminating story about persons whom we need not take to be historical individuals. Zeus and Odin, and Pandora who opened her box of troubles, are mythical characters: also surely Adam and Eve, the first two human beings, created fully-grown from the dust of the earth, who committed the first sin.

The Gospels are evidently not works of *fiction,* tales fashioned for entertainment, tragedies and comedies such as *Hamlet* or *Pride and Prejudice.* Christians may be more concerned about whether the Gospel stories are *legends,* narratives that have started with facts but grown in the telling, such as the travels of Odysseus, the adventures of Robin Hood, Dr. Spooner's verbal tangles, and perhaps indeed the Nativity of Christ in a stable.

But indeed the category where the Gospel records must primarily belong for believers is *history,* narratives of events, needing to be judged as accurate or inaccurate, like accounts of the reign of Queen Elizabeth I or the Battle of Waterloo. Recent New Testament criticism has encouragingly reduced the supposed yawning gap between what really happened and the tradition that the church has received and passed on,[12] convincingly ascribing more to the witness of contemporaries and less to inventive storytelling. The claim is that the Gospel writers were responsible human historians, able to draw upon the testimony of honest eyewitnesses.

To say that they were dependable, even that they were truly *inspired,* does not mean that they were *inerrant.* The fundamentalist notion is misleading, that what they wrote was "the Word of the Lord," dictated from on high without possibility of ignorance, mistake, or misunderstanding. To insist upon that kind of inflexible conviction actually makes it harder for people to find there the credible truth they need.

---

10. Matt 11:30.

11. Mark 2:27.

12. See Dunn, *Jesus Remembered,* and especially Bauckham, *Jesus and the Eyewitnesses.*

Liberal Christians can allow without dismay for some errors of fact and even for some legendary material to have been included, but their commitment is to mainly trustworthy accounts of real happenings. If they say, "Even though we really know very little about Jesus of Nazareth, we *affirm* that the Gospels are good news," they blur the distinction between truth and falsity.

Inquirers who care about truthfulness have reason to be dubious when Christians do not seem to mind much about the historical consistency of their faith. For instance, believers hail the Lord as the Son of David,[13] in the same context as they confidently state that he was not the son of Joseph who was David's descendant. If Christians could bear to be more tentative about whether the conception of Jesus was necessarily miraculous, they could at least affirm that there was a doubt about his parentage, and make a valid theological point about it. The tradition says that Joseph, who was born of David's line, took Mary as his wife and gave recognition to her baby.[14] The adoption of a child is not a deception nor even a fiction. Whether Christians believe or disbelieve that Jesus had no human father, they can welcome the notion that Jesus had King David as his ancestor, maybe not by birthright, but by human grace. They can state that the Son of God was adopted as the son of Joseph and the Son of David, and that likewise human beings can be made sons and daughters of God, not by right, but by divine adoption and grace.[15]

The legends that have gathered around the birth of Jesus Christ in a manger may be both compared and contrasted with the burgeoning Christmas mythology of Santa Claus who comes down chimneys. Telling stories about Father Christmas is a life-enhancing game. "Let's pretend" is an idea that children soon learn to understand well, a happy characteristic part of their upbringing. Their elders join in the annual rituals of expecting a jovial personage to bring presents all the way from Lapland. Sometimes the game gets out of hand, pretence turns into deception, and disillusionment threatens. Santa has lost touch with Saint Nicholas, the long-ago servant of God who practiced Christian charity by giving surprise presents, and has developed into a supernatural figure who travels from afar on Christmas Eve, in a sleigh drawn by reindeer, to fill all the children's stockings, a powerful rival to Baby Jesus in Bethlehem.

13. E.g., Matt 1:1; 16–17; 21:9; Mark 10:48; Luke 18:38–39.
14. Matt 1: 20–21, 24.
15. Rom 8:14–17; Gal 4:4–7.

The story of Jesus, by contrast, is the story of a historical person who was born of a woman in a particular place, on a particular day about two thousand years ago. Whether his birth was in Bethlehem or Nazareth, whether or not it was attended by ox and ass, shepherds and sages, Baby Jesus grew up to be a man. Historians can and must inquire about how he lived and how he died, and why he is worshiped still as Lord Jesus who is the Son of God.

What matters, for Christian belief to be true, is that this man, whose teaching inspired his followers, who was crucified and died, is now alive. It is not just the ideas that he stood for that live on: it is he himself. He came back to his disciples, no wish-fulfilling hallucination but the Risen Lord. The tradition is strong that his tomb was found to be empty on the third day; but the empty tomb does not have to be the whole meaning of the Resurrection, nor even the main meaning. What matters is that Jesus who had died showed himself as alive again and victorious. There should be room in the Christian church for the people who thoroughly believe that the Lord is risen indeed, but who think that what happened to his earthly body that died is not so clear. Christians can argue and wonder, and may arrive at different opinions about the physical character of his resurrection then, and ours at last: but surely without unchurching one another.

7

The Hypothesis of Faith

Walk about Zion, and go round about her:
and tell the towers thereof.
Mark well her bulwarks, set up her houses:
that ye may tell them that come after.

PSALM 48:11–12

THE CHRISTIAN CREEDS STATE that we believe "in one Lord Jesus Christ, the only-begotten Son of God,"[1] who was killed and rose again on the third day. As a way of triumphantly expressing their faith, Christians have liked to quote from the book of Job, "I know that my Redeemer liveth";[2] but some of us are more able to keep saying "I believe," rather than "I know." We are glad to declare, "I confidently trust." We affirm that we expect and hope to see plainly one day that the Christian creeds do indeed tell the truth about the universe. We still cannot claim that we know the truth of Christianity in the same way as we know who we are and where we are. God the Father cannot be seen, nor heard speaking, in the way that creatures can see and hear each other. Nor can we prove that God exists in the way that one can prove a mathematical theorem.

I must therefore state and emphasize, at the risk of shocking some believers, that it is reasonable to embrace the Christian faith as a working hypothesis. It makes a good start to say, *Suppose* this is true; and then to

---

1. The Nicene Creed used in the Communion service (*The Book of Common Prayer, Common Worship*, etc.).

2. Job 19:25.

go on to ask, Does it hang together? Does it explain the known facts better than any other hypothesis? Does it make better and better sense the further one goes? Can I live by it? Belief in the hypothesis of faith depends upon the backing of experience, in something like the way that scientific hypotheses need experimental confirmation.

If faith is rightly taken to have the status of a hypothesis to be tested, it may upsettingly appear that having faith can hardly be the virtue that Christians have supposed. Assuming what one needs to prove is a sinful folly. To be open-minded at first and even uncertain, to adopt this hypothesis cautiously and look for confirmation, is not disloyal but rational. Skeptics are right to refuse to jump to conclusions. On the contrary, people of integrity proportion their beliefs to the evidence. Not many believers are dishonest enough to say, "Never mind whether we know this, but let's anyway tell them it's true." Unfortunately too many believers say something like, "It's not for us to argue. We must simply proclaim the good news."

The ethics of faith cannot be so simple as a plain duty to believe what we are told. More promisingly, there is a virtue of receptiveness, of readiness to appreciate. There is a duty to pay heed, to put one's heart into the effort to understand. Iris Murdoch wrote impressively about the importance of "focusing our attention,"[3] quoting St Paul: "Whatsoever things are true"— honest, just, pure, lovely, of good report—"think on these things."[4] She connects attention with unselfish detachment: "real things can be looked at and loved without being seized and used." Her most telling examples[5] are a bird-watcher whose anxiety and resentment are driven away by noticing a hovering kestrel; and a mother-in-law who learns, by attending, to see her daughter-in-law as not "vulgar but refreshingly simple, not tiresomely juvenile but delightfully youthful . . ."

If the virtue of faith has something to do with attentiveness, unbelief may indeed turn out to be blameworthy, not merely mistaken. What is wrong with it is not a regrettable but surely innocent failure to achieve assurance. If lack of faith is indeed sinful, its fault is a hasty negative assurance, rejecting opportunities to listen and look. Skeptics are not to blame for giving incorrect answers so much as for undervaluing the questions, making over-confident assumptions, avoiding the responsibility of trying to find out, scorning other people's experience.

3. Murdoch, *The Sovereignty of Good*, 56.

4. Phil 4:8.

5. Murdoch, *The Sovereignty of Good*, 56.

Browning's Bishop Blougram pressed the question,[6]

> What think ye of Christ, friend? When all's done and said,
> Like you this Christianity or not?
> It may be false but will you wish it true?
> Has it your vote to be so if it can?

He is not saying, "Take your choice: believe what you feel like," but, "Make your choice: which side will you back?" If this news would be good news, it claims responsible attention. I may not be accountable for what beliefs I happen to have acquired, but I am responsible for giving priority to what matters.

Christian faith matters because it addresses urgent questions which human beings ask. When a philosopher sets up a definition of God as, say, "omniscient, omnipotent, and omnipresent,"[7] he cannot be blamed for proceeding to argue for his inference that there can be no such Being. But if he is contented to have arrived at the academic conclusion that something, some *thing* called God, happens not to exist, just as he is contented to agree that unicorns do not exist, one may wonder whether he has seen the point of the inquiry. When people are asking painful questions about the troubles of the world, the hypothesis that there is a good Creator who will set things right at last ought not to be coolly set aside. Of course I am not obliged to believe it no matter what. I am obliged not to write off this hope indifferently.

Christian believers take sides with Christ, and taking sides is a combination of conviction and response. Gibbon[8] tells that King Clovis, on being converted, was instructed in the story of the Crucifixion and exclaimed, "with indiscreet fury, 'Had I been present at the head of my valiant Franks, I would have revenged his injuries.'" Though we agree that he got it wrong, we may still feel that faith as warm-hearted partisanship looks more like a virtue than the kind of intellectual ratiocination that neutrally weighs up the arguments for and against the existence of a God, without much caring what the upshot will be.

Giving Christianity my vote, to be true if it can, does not mean claiming final assurance in this life; but adopting this stance and seeking more enlightenment. Just because I so much want this to be true, I must not take it for granted. I am in a somewhat similar position to a counsel for the

---

6. Browning, "Bishop Blougram's Apology," *Poems*, vol. I, 617–42.

7. E.g., Shand, "A Refutation of the Existence of God," 63.

8. Gibbon, *Decline and Fall of the Roman Empire*, vol. 4, 116.

defense, whose effectiveness depends upon taking the opposing case seriously, not neutral indeed but not prejudiced, looking honestly at the data in the way that scientists learn to do.

To take sides on behalf of faith is far from taking sides against science, as if a scientific viewpoint were evidently hostile to religion. How could science and faith be foes, if faith states rightly that the universe that scientists explore is God's creation? The qualities the study of science demands are honesty, humility, open-mindedness, realism, energy, patience, attentiveness, and indeed a kind of reverence. Surely these are also the qualities faith needs. Real scientists do not deaden the universe they are examining on the contrary. They enlarge, not shrink, the human capacity for enthrallment. They may admit into their worldview, as Immanuel Kant did into his philosophy, with "ever increasing wonder and awe," "the starry heavens above and the moral law within."[9]

Whatever else schoolchildren are taught nowadays, the physical sciences are likely to be have a major place; and it makes sense to start where people are. That does not mean that one must stop there. Suppose that the natural world, however magnificent and fascinating, really is not all there is. What can someone who entertains that hypothesis say to inquirers young and old about God, the Creator of the natural world? What, or rather Who, is there, to elicit our wonder? Christians reply to that question, "We have learned to believe in God, who is Father, Son, and Holy Spirit."

When they tell their complex story about the Lord their God, why trust them? For some people, faith does look obvious. God is Somebody they know as plainly as they know their friends, inspiring their lives, guiding their actions, or maybe pursuing them relentlessly like the Hound of Heaven. Such straightforward piety is honorable, indeed impressive, and is not to be hastily written off as credulity; though it cannot be expected to attract or convince everyone. Belief in God cannot be established simply by bare statements of confident faith. Believers must set out the evidence that supports the hypothesis of a reality beyond the limited horizon of the world in which we live. Their data consist of the written reports of *scripture*, the continuing experience of *tradition*, and the conclusions people reach by using their *reason*.

Especially for someone whose academic starting point was philosophy, the roles of inquirer about God and believer in God are plaited together. The kind of philosophy I was taught in my youth was much concerned with

9. Kant, *Critique of Practical Reason*, 163.

the difference between belief and knowledge.[10] The sort of thing we really knew was that 2 + 2 = 4. It was also in order to be entirely sure that when I sit at my desk I feel and see a hard brown surface broken by colored patches. But then I had to ask: Do I know, or merely suppose, that this brown shape is the top of a solid piece of furniture that is still there when I am in another room? We had to wonder seriously whether we *know* anything we cannot either calculate or experience at first hand. Are other people real and conscious like me? Will the sun rise tomorrow? Is morality as plain as it seems? Can we state as a fact that hurting people is wrong? Why believe in God? These all presented themselves as live questions in a branch of analytical philosophy called "theory of knowledge." We had to be careful to distinguish knowing, not only from believing, but from supposing, assuming, taking for granted . . .

Doubting Thomas, who needed to see and touch for himself, would make a good patron saint.[11] Our prophet was Descartes, from whom we learnt to doubt everything we possibly could, in order to see clearly whether anything remained undeniable at last.[12] We studied the British empiricists, Locke, Berkeley, and Hume, who taught us to inspect our commonsense certainties. To start as skeptics was not a sin but a duty. Among all this mid-twentieth-century philosophizing, the question whether faith in God can or cannot be upheld as rational impressed itself permanently upon those of us who aspired to be Christians.

To distinguish between knowing, believing, positing, and jumping to conclusions is more than an intriguing exercise. The difference between sound and unsound thinking matters morally. Faith accordingly faces the charge of culpable dishonesty, for making assertions that go beyond the evidence. To argue without due care and attention is to run the risk of being overturned by reality, misled myself and misleading other people.

Among many valid vocations for Christians, scholarship is one. For somebody who is aware of such a calling, integrity forces the question: Must there be a battle between reason and faith? If they seem to pull in different ways, a Christian scholar needs to show that Christian faith is compatible with loyalty to reason. I must say more than that: responsible faith needs to be positively founded upon loyalty to reason.

10. See, e.g., Broad, *The Mind and Its Place in Nature*; Price, *Perception,* e.g., 139–42; Russell, *The Problems of Philosophy*; and Buford, ed., *Essays on Other Minds.*

11. John 14:5, 20, 25.

12. Descartes, *Discourse on Method.*

The precept that belief ought to be proportioned to the evidence belongs to the elementary ethic of scholarship. I am content with this, because I happen to dislike gambling and tend to look on risk as alarming. Scholarly caution about what beliefs I should accept is not faithless. It must be irresponsible to plump for faith, to throw myself into faith and to allow myself to think wishfully what I hope is true. Believing can look too much like the sort of compulsion that rational people call addiction. This horse is bound to win this time because it would be so satisfying if it did. Far from such confidence having authority, it ought to be avoided as a temptation.

Christian faith is no foregone conclusion. I have to carry on the argument with myself and others about why I believe. Honesty or stubbornness makes me keep asking, am I arguing fairly or unfairly? I cannot make faith true by voting for it. I am not an elector choosing which candidate shall be the winner, but more like a member of a jury, required to consider the evidence and give a responsible verdict about the alleged facts. Having tried hard to judge fairly, I assert that the case has been made out and that faith does indeed win the argument. More humbly perhaps, I find that "this Christianity"[13] does claim my allegiance.

13. See pp. 49 above and note 6.

8

Rational Inquiry

We shall trust him, if he exists, but we can
hardly trust him to exist. We must have reason
to think that he does.

AUSTIN FARRER (1966), 10

LOOKING FOR ARGUMENTS IN favor of believing may seem an elitist
inquiry. Faith is supposed to be for everyone, not only for brainy
people who weigh up evidence. Practical Christians may have a feeling
that this intellectual caution is taking a wrong turning. Can the safety of
my soul depend upon the careful calculation of probabilities? Cool assess-
ment of pros and cons easily becomes legalistic, indeed self-righteous, and
even mean-spirited. The scholarly duty to found faith upon reason remains
insistent, but there is more to reason than following arguments. Ratiocination is merely one way to arrive at truth, not the only way. Wisdom is not
reducible to careful computation.

Does the balance need redressing still further? Commonsense making judgments by habit and instinct may be more reliable than intellect
moving step by step. Perhaps those of us who like to be on the safe side,
who want to be thoroughly protected from risks, are not being responsible,
just faint-hearted. We may fairly be told, "Don't be so negative about the
kind of faith that is a generous gamble." Of course betting is dangerous
and some people get addicted to it, just as some become addicted to "wine

that maketh glad the heart of man."[1] But people whose actual temptation is to insist nervously on safety might be encouraged to stop considering so sedately where they stand. They might allow themselves to embark upon faith as a venture, not looking for full certainty before they dare commit themselves, but encouraged by what they have understood so far and finding confirmation as they go on.

People make free choices, quite different from addiction, to take risks that they judge to be worthwhile. There is the little flutter, the charity raffle, which is harmless fun. There are big risks too that good human beings find themselves bound to take. They change their jobs, they move house, they join campaigns, they set off into the wilderness; and often they turn out to have been right not to heed the kindly warnings. Even if in the end they fail, they may be glad to have tried. That seems a more appealing account of faith than relentless ratiocination.

Some of us will go on feeling happier with reasoning than with risk; but surprising as it may seem, the gospel of Christ seems to favor generous gambling more than careful appraisal. The Lord characteristically praises bold faith. Someone seeking the kingdom is like a merchant selling everything to buy one pearl;[2] people's faith makes them whole; fishermen "immediately" abandon their boats to follow Christ.[3] St. Paul's converts are justified by faith rather than by works. The message sometimes seems to be, "Have a fling.'"

Cautious people will not like this. They find themselves agreeing, however reluctantly, not with the brave but hasty Christians, but with the vigilant skeptics who are ready to accuse believers of foolish and unprincipled self-indulgence. When unbelief presents itself as truthful and mature, it is self-assured faith that finds itself on trial. Believers have to face a moral indictment, that they are trying to make piety a substitute for good sense. The prosecuting judges are not persecuting tyrants, but familiar congenial contemporaries.

Christians are used to the charge, not always unfair, that their loyalty appears narrow and intolerant and that their morality is not sublime but negative and life-denying. Nowadays they are confronted by a still more basic ethical assault. However kindly they live, their practice of charity will not help them to refute the allegation that the faith they profess is based

---

1. Ps 104:15.

2. Matt 13:45–46.

3. Matt 4:18–22; Mark 1:16–20.

on irrational assumptions. Their splendid venture is not so splendid if its intellectual foundations are insecure.

Faith faces a two-pronged onslaught, under attack as both dishonest and naive. If the doctrine that good Christians preach looks too much like wishful thinking, their confidence will not be excused as innocent folly, but blamed as a culpable offense against truth. It is not a good enough response to ignore this attack and go ahead unthinkingly with obedient piety.

Citizens of God's kingdom find themselves also subject to the moral authority of human ethical understanding. "Obey God rather than men"?[4]—yes indeed; but obedience to God expressly requires them to pay heed to one another. The plain decision to serve God is far from justifying a disregard for other people's moral integrity. Divine and human moral claims are tangled together. Only reconciliation will do.

At least the laws of the two jurisdictions overlap and their demands may coincide. Christian ethics and secular ethics both take truth to be a fundamental value. In the fourth Gospel in particular, truth is a keyword, strongly underlined by the Lord's announcement that he himself in person is the Way, the Truth, and the Life.[5] A skeptic may find this unacceptably metaphysical, but the holiness it claims for truth is as important as any moralist could wish.

Loyalty to truth as the secular obligation to be honest, whether or not one's favorite insights carry conviction, is more prosaic but no less basic. There is real convergence here about what matters morally, which should allow believers and skeptics to respect one another although they disagree; but their paths cannot go the same way for long.

Believers and unbelievers diverge. They have to part at the place where Christians find themselves obliged to receive gratefully the statements of the faith which was once delivered to the saints.[6] If faith forbids them to explore with an open mind, not knowing what truth they may find, it looks as if faith is awarding priority to piety over truth. On the one hand, believers claim the high moral ground and set up belief itself as the essential Christian virtue. Skeptics, on the contrary, can hardly accept that belief is virtuous at all. Surely assurance is something that may happen to me or may fail to happen? To accept a proposed statement as true is not a demand that I ought to set about meeting by willpower. If I have

4. Acts 5:29.
5. John 14:6.
6. Jude 3.

faith, it looks more seemly to count myself fortunate, rather than to think that I have done my duty.

I may be told that such a neutral position concedes too much to doubt. Religious people cannot readily give up their conviction that faith is a moral choice, moral in the way that pledging one's allegiance is a moral undertaking. They are permitted, indeed obliged, to count deciding for faith as an ethical responsibility.

Bernard Shaw announced[7] provocatively that "belief is literally a matter of taste." If it is even partly correct that people are accountable for what they believe, it follows that beliefs are on the way to being praiseworthy or blameworthy. People cannot be confident after all that they can do their whole duty by pursuing the argument wherever it may lead, being honest about where it has led them so far, and being fair to people who think otherwise. They find themselves morally obliged not to sit on the fence but to take sides.

It is impossible to read the Gospels and ignore their overwhelming emphasis on faith, not apparently reason, as a main criterion for making moral judgments. The New Testament even makes a point of praising what looks like blind faith. Disciples are told, "Do not fear, only believe."[8] It may look as if making the right assumptions, affirming the right doctrines, matters more for Christians than doing the right acts. If this claim is taken seriously, it cuts shockingly across our best human moral understanding. Followers of Christ know, of course, that their faith may challenge them to make great sacrifices of their human concerns for the sake of the gospel, even to forsake "house or brothers or sisters or mother or father or lands";[9] but surely it cannot be right to include their intellectual integrity among the good things which the gospel may ask them heroically to renounce.

The other prong of the skeptical onslaught, the accusation of naive folly, can no more be brushed aside than the allegation of dishonesty. According to the Gospel teaching, it seems, caution is to be abandoned and risk-taking is positively commendable. If a poor widow casts all her livelihood into the treasury, we are to be delighted by her generosity, not alarmed by her imprudence.[10] When James and John heard the Lord's call,

7. Shaw, *Androcles and the Lion*, 510.

8. Mark 5:36.

9. Mark 10:29.

10. Mark 12:42.

they promptly left their aged father in the boat and obeyed the command.[11] Is it irreverent to wonder whether such precipitate haste might be thoughtless or even unkind, surely not an example of how Christians ought to behave? Though a believer can point out defensively that Zebedee had the hired servants to look after him, the feeling lingers that to offer this vivid picture from the days in Galilee as a lesson for all disciples, to set up unquestioning obedience as a basic moral standard, is not really a promising way for Christians to practice or commend their faith.

The New Testament demand for unconditional commitment cannot silence the human voice of conscientious thought. Unless they can be reconciled, we might have to call faith unethical. St. Augustine as a responsible Christian bishop did not commend but sternly reproved a member of his flock for trustfully giving large sums of money to two vagrants, upsetting her pagan husband who had been a promising convert.[12] When simple faith verges upon simple foolishness, it can hardly claim moral authority.

Christians must heed these reproaches, but need not be too daunted to defend themselves. At least they can repudiate the charge that Christianity requires blind compliance. They are not obliged to shut their eyes and plunge into credulity. When Doubting Thomas declined to make a leap of faith, he was not blamed: he was greeted by the Risen Christ.[13] Nor does faith demand irresponsible heedlessness. Disciples are not forbidden to "count the cost": on the contrary. "For which of you, desiring to build a tower, does not first"—do what?—"sit down and"—indeed—"count the cost."[14]

A favorite defense of faith, which may still be glib if it is trotted out hastily, is to emphasize the distinction between believing *that*, governed by logic, and believing *in*, governed by loyalty. We must first use our reason to formulate belief *that*; then go on faithfully to practice belief *in*. When we trust somebody, the loyalty we owe is founded upon the conviction we have reached, which in itself is morally neutral, that our confidence is based upon true statements.

It is not so easy to make this separation in practice. Among all the faithful people we know or read about, can we sort out which of them are commendably putting their trust *in* their God, and which of them are merely fortunate to have no doubt *that* what they have been told about God

11. Matt 4:22; Mark 1:20.

12. Augustine, Epistle CCLXII, *Select Letters*, 507–9.

13. John 20:24–29.

14. Luke 14:28–31.

is true? Othello's belief that Desdemona loves him and his faith in Desdemona belong to one moral commitment that cannot be taken apart so that he can establish *this* first; and then *that* will clearly follow. Both succumb together to Iago's assault. His situation is truly tragic, because he is neither simply blameless for losing his belief, nor simply wrong for desperately abandoning his trust.

Rather than conceding that since people cannot control their beliefs, lack of faith cannot be a sin, it looks tempting to rescue the virtue of faith by defining faith differently, adjusting its plain meaning in order to allow piety to be praiseworthy. Instead of approving of intellectual conviction as such, however shaky the arguments for reaching it, people identify the moral meaning of faith, which makes it a virtue, as *faithfulness*, living loyally by whatever faith one holds. Instead of supposing that believers are saved by happening to judge rightly which dogmas to accept or deny, we can evidently hold them responsible for what they do about their beliefs. At least steadfastness is a good part of what Christians mean by the virtue of faith: not turning back once I have put my hand to the plough.[15] If this account would serve, it would obviate any dubious obligation either to force myself to believe, or to make positive declarations without being truly convinced. Better still, faithful Christians could thankfully stop being so intolerant of other people's honest doubt.

So far, so good: but there remains a lingering feeling that to settle for defining Christian faith as faithfulness is cheating. If I look up "faith" in a concordance, I cannot find the message, "people who are lucky enough to have faith ought to put it into practice." I find the Lord praising people for having faith; and still more tellingly rebuking them for lacking it.[16] St. Paul is at the heart of an immense controversy when he gives *having* faith priority over *doing* good works. It cannot be enough just to hope for the blessing of faith and then pursue it loyally if it does come my way. Since it appears that I am obliged to be active in taking steps to achieve faith, what steps am I bound to take?

If *having faith* is as important as Christian teaching claims, the believing that matters so greatly must amount to more than careful honest thinking that has happily arrived at a positive conclusion. The faith that is a basic virtue alongside hope and charity cannot be reduced to a mental exercise of which some are capable and some are incapable. Criticizing

15. Luke 9:62.

16. E.g., Matt 8:26; 14:31.

people's faith or lack of faith must be more weighty than criticizing the effectiveness of their intellectual processes. The criterion for having the kind of faith that qualifies people as real Christians cannot be, Have they argued correctly?—nor even, Have they taken enough trouble to find out whether the right answer is Yes, No, or Perhaps? Their moral accountability for their convictions does include reasoning as accurately as they can; but they are more deeply responsible than that.

Honest faith includes exactness and diligence; but for faith to be the essential virtue Christians suppose, the ethics of belief needs to be understood more ambitiously, beyond the ordinary responsibility for being careful. Thinking people seem to be somehow accountable, not only for whether they carry out their mental operations conscientiously, but for their attitude of mind, their hopes, the point of view they adopt towards what they trying to discover. People can be praised or blamed for what they seek and hope to find. If we say that they have *good* judgment, we are generally ascribing to them not only intelligence but also moral qualities like empathy, sensitivity, and generosity, which add up to wisdom.

The difference between neutral belief *that* and loyal belief *in* is still a valid preliminary distinction. There is a recognizable difference between what merely happens to someone and what someone positively does. To find oneself convinced *that* something is or is not the case may be no credit or fault; but what is morally required of human beings is not perfunctory acknowledgement but appropriate response. Putting one's faith in *somebody* is a commitment to fidelity, which does entail something like casting one's vote.[17] If belief in God is admirable rather than just fortunate, it begins with thorough honest attention and comes to be expressed by taking sides.

I cannot speak for everyone, but I have to affirm my own faith. The Christian story that God entered human life claims my allegiance, because I find here an answer that I can believe to the questions I have to ask. The gospel of Christ who suffered and rose from death provides needful support for the hypothesis that the universe is God's beloved creation. The hypothesis matters: if it is true that there is a God who is on our side, it is indeed good news. Surely there is no sin in disbelieving the gospel, but it must be wrong either to deny it unconcernedly, or to believe it but take no notice.

Jesus Christ does not have to be the only starting point for true belief in God. He could not be, because Christian faith was built on Jewish faith. Rather, he is the keystone of the arch: the stone that once put in place binds

17. See above, Chapter 7, 49, 52.

the whole structure firmly together.[18] Oddly enough, many believers do not seem to worry about how the structure of faith holds up. But the question arises insistently for some, How can a good God have made this universe?

Human miseries are the hard data that count against the Christian hypothesis about God. In a good creation, one might expect human experience to be challenging and even arduous; but many people's lives are grim. They may well find it more likely that the whole course of history has happened by chance and that there is no God at all. Since people do not accept authority readily today, they are free to persist in asking the urgent question, What right had God to make a world like this?[19] The keystone that holds up the Christian faith is the conviction that the Creator took the responsibility by entering human life and bearing the burden.

18. Ps 118:22; Acts 4:11; Eph 2:20.

19. See above, Chapter 5, e.g., 34, 39.

9

Gospel Story

This good God,—what he could do if he would,
Would, if he could—then must have done long since:
If so, when, where and how? Some way must be,—
Once feel about, and soon or late you hit
Some sense, in which it might be, after all.
Why not, "The Way, the Truth and the Life"?

ROBERT BROWNING, "BISHOP BLOUGRAM'S APOLOGY"

UNLESS BELIEVERS CAN OFFER beginners a reasonable account of what the gospel of Christ means and why it is trustworthy, they will have to send learners out into the world clutching their faith like a brightly colored balloon, which will burst as soon a pin is stuck in it.[1] When children ask hard questions, it is not good enough to tell them to wait until they are old enough to understand. Who is old enough to comprehend God? Who is too young to make a start? The story that God found it worthwhile to suffer for the sake of creation may seem difficult and not important to teach to children; but the questions people ask do not depend much upon how old they are. "Why did God let my rabbit die?" is an authentic example of the adult problem of evil. It is unfair to children who have begun to realize that animals and people get hurt, and to the people these children will grow up to be, if they are taught to praise a God who has never been hurt.

1. I discussed the question of presenting the Christian faith to children in *Helping Children Find God.*

61

Adults are tempted to restrict children to a limited version of Christian faith. They keep the difficult parts of the story for later on and put all the emphasis on Christmas, which is a happy story about a new baby and comfortable animals around the crib. So far, so good: but not far enough. To stop at the stable in Bethlehem is to miss what matters about the gospel. Christmas celebrates the coming of God into human life, but Christmas on its own is only an introduction to the story. It is Good Friday that shows that God is on our side. It is Easter that shows that God can cope.

Of course the brutal Cross is unsuitable for children. Meanwhile life's troubles are obvious, on television and nearer home. Unless people have been taught as children what Christians believe about God meeting the cost of making this complex and wonderful universe, it is not surprising that when something dreadful happens adults wonder why God has abandoned them and find it natural to abandon belief in God.

Here is a summary version of Christian teaching, which unfortunately is not altogether a caricature: God made everything in six days. God told people about right and wrong. They did wrong and God was angry, but agreed to punish Jesus instead. Jesus is very good and wants us to keep telling him so. If we ask him nicely he will always look after us. One day, if we are good, our souls will go to heaven with all the other good people's souls, but no teddy bears or dogs and no bad people. We do not talk about heaven much in everyday life, because people's bare souls are embarrassing, just as people's bare bodies are embarrassing.

We should do better to try this: The universe is marvelous and God made it. God does not arrange everything that happens in it like producing a play, but allows creatures to live their lives, in a world that turns out to be a mixture of happiness and misery. God knows it all and minds about it all. Especially God minds about people. A lot has gone wrong, and a lot of what has gone wrong is people's own fault, but God does not keep blaming them and saying, "Look what you have done." God came into the world to be a human being like us, so God knows at first hand what human life is like; and we can trust God to work out the happy ending for us at last.

"God was in Christ reconciling the world to himself."[2] Had it been possible for the good universe to continue unshaken by troubles and free from transgressions, would the God who made it have entered into human life anyway and lived and died serenely to show us the way? Even in our difficult world, if the chosen people had been ready, as a community, to

2. 2 Cor 5:19.

take on their role of welcoming the Christ when he came,[3] might the cost of creation have been less dreadful than crucifixion?

The Christian understanding of the data we have is that the Son of God became a human being in order to take responsibility for the world as it is. He needed to live as a mortal creature and experience the reality of human life at its worst, which included the fear of dying,[4] the hurt of betrayal,[5] the pain of violent death, and the desolation of losing touch with God.[6] There was no cheating. Christians in distress need not think bitterly, "It's all very well for God."

Austin Farrer used to ask the question whether Jesus knew plainly all along that he was God, and applied a distinction made by Gilbert Ryle,[7] to suggest that the Lord's human consciousness might not give him knowledge *that* but knowledge *how*. He did not need to say to himself "I am the second Person of the Trinity." He knew how to be God living a human life. The perfect man found out for himself what earthly enjoyment and pleasure are like, and then disappointment and defeat, with no last-minute rescue. As God-made-human, he had the experience of painfully aligning his human wishes with the will of God.[8]

It is part of the story that the Lord did not avoid the ordinary daunting human trial of wanting to do what he ought not. The account of his ordeal in the wilderness[9] is shaped as an encounter with Satan in person, which can well be understood as mythical. We may take the notion of evil appearing in bodily form to be a figure of speech. What remains in bare prose is not a legend but a historical story about the experience of a man really tempted to do what he knew he could have done well. He set aside the idea of ruling the world gloriously and undertook instead to save the world divinely.

In Luke's Gospel the story of the temptations concludes with the ominous statement that the devil left him "for a season."[10] Later there follows

---

3. Matt 23:37.

4. Matt 26:36–38; Mark 14:33–34; Luke 22:44.

5. Matt 26:14, 25, 49–50; Mark 14:10, 43; Luke 22:3, 47–48; John 6:71; 13:2, 26; 18: 2–6.

6. Matt 27:46; Mark 15:34.

7. Ryle, *The Concept of Mind*, 25–61.

8. Matt 26:38–39; Mark 14:34–36; Luke 22:42–44.

9. Matt 4:8–9; Mark 1:13; Luke 4:5–7.

10. Luke 4:13 (King James Version).

the account of how the Apostle St. Peter became Satan's mouthpiece, loyally protesting "God forbid it, Lord!"[11] at the dreadful prospect of the Passion. The sharp rebuke of Jesus, "Get behind me, Satan," reveals to any hardpressed discile to this day, more plainly than any gentle reproach, the human strain which the Lord had to face.

The doctrine that God's Son came to live among us, experiencing the restrictions of human life, can be explored with the help of the frivolous image that the human world he entered is like an aquarium, where light comes in but the reality outside is hidden from sight. The impertinence of comparing the Lord God with a fish in a tank can encourage a reflection that is not so frivolous, the wonder of the statement that the Almighty did cross the divide between the Creator and every creature. The incongruity is salutary, if Christians are tempted to take it for granted that of course it is in order to identify a particular finite human person as an appropriate image of God.

Rather than trying to do without metaphorical language and to speak literally about their faith, believers may humbly realize that even inadequate analogies can serve to illuminate their ideas of Deity. Without relying idolatrously upon any one notion of what God is like, they can combine assorted similes: a mother hen,[12] a mighty warrior,[13] a sculptor shaping a man out of clay.[14] The purpose of using imagery is to point towards the elusive literal idea that as a matter of fact there is a Power who did bring the universe into being and who entered at a particular time into an individual human life, in order to be "God with us." It would not be surprising for this gospel to be rejected as too good to be true; but it is odd that people ignore it as too boring to be worth the effort of considering it.

Christians believe the good news that earthly troubles are not everlasting and that in the end God will bring everything to good. What they say to back this up is, indeed, *crucial*: their hope depends upon the Cross. They do not suppose that God indifferently brought a world full of people into being and serenely lets them suffer, saying "I will sort it out, all in good time." They can sum up their faith briefly: the Creator painfully paid the price because the cost is worthwhile. Christians who have had to realize that good people may have miserable experiences are able to say, "God

11. Matt 16:22–23.

12. Matt 23:37.

13. E.g., Pss 9, 44, 45, 68, 72.

14. Gen 2:7.

understands the risk, and God has joined in with us." The serene faith of the Psalmist who had never seen the righteous forsaken[15] is contradicted by the cry of desolation in Psalm 22; and that cry turned out to be a prophecy of the Lord's human experience when he came.[16]

But then, unless the dying God is also the rising God, the story ends catastrophically with defeat and failure. That could be noble and inspiring; but it would provide no moral justification for the creation of such a hazardous world. It is not enough for disciples to find some meaning in the tragic tale which makes them feel better. "If Christ has not been *raised*, your faith is futile."[17] Without both the disaster of the Cross and the triumph of the Resurrection, the data would be lacking to support responsible faith in a good God.

Did Jesus really rise after he died? People who would like to follow him, but who suppose that no thinking person today can believe in miracles, try to do without belief in his literal rising. He died, his human experience came to an end, his body was buried and saw corruption, but his disciples recognized and still recognize his Spirit living on in their hearts. If Christians reduce his risen life in this kind of way to heavenly inspiration for believers, without anything in particular happening to Jesus himself, they are surely being defeatist.[18] The stories about the empty tomb may perhaps be later and less basic than the stories about the Lord's appearances to his disciples, but there would be no gospel without some special happening on the first Easter Day. Christians affirm that the Father acted decisively to vindicate the Son: "Now is Christ risen from the dead and become the first fruits of them that slept."[19]

People who believe in God and look on nature as God's creation have already given up plain materialism. They cannot suppose that physics can comprehend the universe fully as a closed, self-sufficient and predictable mechanical system. Granted the huge proviso that there is indeed enough reason for saying, "We believe in God," room can be found in the history

15. Ps 37:25.

16. Matt 27:46 and Mark 15:34.

17. 1 Cor 15:17.

18. See Dunn, *Jesus Remembered*, Chapter 18. He argues carefully that "it is the impact summarized in the word 'resurrection' which requires us to conclude that there was a something which happened 'on the third day,'" . . . "something perceived as having happened to *Jesus* . . . and not just something which happened to the *disciples*" (876). See Oppenheimer, *The Hope of Heaven*, Chapters 8 and 9.

19. 1 Cor 15:20.

of the world for the kind of specific mind-stretching divine action that the Gospels recount.

Christian philosophers who have sat at the feet of David Hume[20] may suppose that tales of wonders, far from confirming their faith, ought indeed to make rational people more doubtful. Hume affably acknowledges that a marvel violating the ordinary course of nature might possibly turn out to be so well attested that it had to be accepted;[21] but he is much more sure of the unreliability of human testimony, particularly about matters of faith. People love a good story. A miracle therefore must always be the less likely explanation and "can never be proved, so as to be the foundation of a system of religion."[22] "Our most holy religion is founded on *Faith,* not on reason."[23] With amiable irony, Hume asserts that miracles may indeed happen. What he finds truly miraculous is the determination of the believer to assent to something "which subverts all the principles of his understanding."[24]

Rather than giving way to despondency or to indignation, and rather than submitting to the notion that faith belongs in a compartment of its own, safely out of reach of argument, Christians should choose instead to follow some biblical advice, which was not devised by an academic in an ivory tower, but is ascribed to a Galilean fisherman.[25] "Always be prepared to make a defense to anyone who calls you to account for the hope that is in you, yet do it with gentleness and reverence." Christians ought to be ready to back up their belief with reasons. Sound faith is not excitable credulity, nor stubborn obstinacy, but realistic loyalty to the best insights one can gather, based on honest thinking or on firsthand experience. To trust the testimony of other people demands responsible attention to what they have to say.

The question is not, "Can we leave out the fairy stories and keep belief in God?" but "Were these witnesses trustworthy? Does the whole picture make sense? Would our God do mighty works?" The answer I am happy to give is that special miracles, especially the miracles recounted in the Gospels, do make sense, provided that they are indeed special not commonplace. In particular, the one basic miracle of the Resurrection does make sense. Piety does not say "Wow!" but, "Yes of course. Now I see." The

20. Hume, "Of Miracles," Section X.

21. Ibid., II, 99.

22. Ibid.

23. Ibid., II, 100.

24. Ibid., II, 101.

25. 1 Pet 3:15.

Creator is not to be expected to intervene intermittently with the ordinary course of nature, but miracles may be recognized as exceptional mighty works clustered around God's coming to live among us.

Hume's attack is effective against miracles that are magical marvels. Supernatural conjuring tricks are the kind of wonder that Christians need not be concerned to defend. The Lord declined to prove his credentials in that way: "I am God—I will now show you—*wham!*" The way his life, culminating in his Rising, verifies the Christian faith is more complex than that. It is indeed more like new data suggesting and confirming a novel scientific hypothesis.

For someone whose mind is not set against any reality beyond the material world, a miracle that finds its place as the focal point of a coherent narrative can shed its initial unlikelihood and become a significant part of the evidence in favor of a proposed worldview. The special power of Jesus to heal the sick was all of a piece with the singular impression his life and teaching made upon his followers. "No man ever spoke like this man."[26] They began to ask, "Who is this?"[27] Could he be the Christ? When his life ended in shameful failure and agony, that hypothesis appeared to be refuted and their dawning hopes extinguished. But death could not hold him and they came to recognize his rising as the fulfillment of God's promises and the manifestation of God's glory. The accounts of how their frightened disappointment gave way to wonder carry conviction, more convincing than the skeptical supposition that careless sensation-mongers set about concocting a marvelous improbable tale and spread it around among credulous people, so effectively that it is still believed today.

The story of how God's love for human creatures is expressed in the life, death, and rising of Christ is not the whole story of what Christians believe. The hypothesis of the Christian gospel is more comprehensive than that. Christians affirm that Jesus is God with us: but this creed has to be expanded. There is more to God than Jesus. People who teach Christianity to children owe it to their pupils not to bypass the doctrine of the Trinity. It is a difficult paradox that God is Three in One: but not more paradoxical than some of the ideas they have to learn about the natural world in their science lessons. If they see the point of studying physics, the difficulty of physics can positively encourage them to be undaunted by the difficulty of theology.

26. John 7:46; and see Matt 7:28–29, Mark 1:22, 27; Luke 4:36.

27. E.g., Matt 21:10; Luke 7:49.

An inquirer can begin to comprehend religious statements by considering what questions he or she is trying to answer. Christians offer the doctrine of the Cross of Christ, the suffering God, as an answer to the question whether God the Creator minds about human distress. They offer the doctrine of the Trinity, the threefold God, as an answer to questions which are likewise not sophisticated, although they lead into deep problems. Did the Creator sit unmoved in heaven above, watching while Jesus was killed? Did Jesus know all along that everything was going to be all right? How can we say that Jesus is with us today? As soon as his followers try to explain, they need the idea that God is both One and Three.

Theology paradoxically presents, not simply three alternative descriptions of the one God, but one image of three united Persons. The Christian insistence on affirming such a complicated account of a threefold God is more important than a theological postscript. This doctrine of the Trinity is needed to sustain the basic statement that the Creator's nature is Love. Just as the best way of life for human creatures is indeed to love *one another*, so the life of God is not a solitary existence on high, out of reach of such mutual relating.

If God were simply One and all alone, the only love that could apply to God's heavenly life would be self-love. In order to have somebody to love unselfishly and reciprocally, the One God would need people, like a lonely old lady who needs a pet animal. But on the hypothesis that God's own being includes distinct Persons loving one another, then God does not have to make a universe in order to start loving.[28] Human beings are extra. God does not need us, but God wants us.[29] We are generously invited to join in God's life.

The first Christians were loyal believers in the Lord their God, who became convinced that one particular man belonged on both sides of the line between the one God and humanity. He had the authority to represent God to human beings and human beings to God. Confronted by the life, death, and rising of Jesus, his disciples discovered that God is more mysterious than they had realized. "God is One" is true but too simple. Einstein's upheaval of Newton's physics provides an illustration of the way a good

28. See Oppenheimer, *Helping Children Find God*, Chapter 18; and *On Being Someone*, 135–36.

29. See Oppenheimer, *On Being Someone*, 136; and *The Hope of Happiness*.

satisfying interim explanation of reality needs to be made more complicated, and indeed mind-boggling, when new data emerge to unsettle it.[30]

The theological hypothesis I have been trying to explain has been called the social theory of the Trinity. It puts the emphasis on the three Persons related to one another, as the most illuminating way to speak of God's love. People who would rather begin by emphasizing the One may summarize their faith more simply, by saying that our one God can be imagined in three ways: as the Father above us, the Son beside, us and the Spirit within us. Whatever human beings try to say about God must be picture language, of course: the baby-talk by which God's children learn to put their notions into words.

Belief that the One God is Father, Son, and Spirit is the distinctive Christian belief, where Christianity differs from other faiths. Christians must come to terms with the idea that faiths do differ and take hold of what is special about their own, if they are not going to relax in a sort of generalized spirituality too vague to amount to much. For Christians who make the effort to reckon with theology, the doctrine of the Trinity can even turn out to make understanding easier, not more difficult. When they set about explaining their faith to fellow human beings who are willing to listen, Christians can offer the idea that love is built into God's own life, which is going on anyway whatever people are thinking about it.

Some Christians find that the Spirit seems the most elusive of the three Persons of the Trinity. Others on the contrary find that the most vividly real faith is the kind that is called "charismatic." What matters to them is their distinctive experience of the Holy Spirit in their lives; and indeed much of the New Testament supports them. These exuberant Christians may feel dissatisfied with everything I am able to say about God as Three in One. Am I leaving out the enlivening Power that really matters? The best I can do is respect their enthusiasm and put it aside, as something which means a great deal to these fellow believers. I must explain as well as I can what matters most to me and hope that other people can expand my partial account into a fuller one.

At least a Christian who finds the third Person of the Trinity hard to imagine can be helped to take heed of the Spirit by biblical imagery. "Spirit" in Hebrew and Greek means both "wind" and "breath"[31] and has to do with in*spir*ation. The creative wind moved over the face of the waters when the

---

30. See Oppenheimer, *On Being Someone,* 32, 137.

31. E.g., John 3:8, and cf. Ezek 37:7–10.

earth was without form and void.[32] The risen Lord breathed on his disciples and said, "Receive the Holy Spirit";[33] and when the day of Pentecost had fully come, a rushing mighty wind filled all the house and descended upon them in tongues of fire.[34]

A traditional image, which is, indeed, enlightening, is to imagine the Spirit as light. Today one can compare the Spirit with the headlights of a car, which illuminate the road ahead but cannot be gazed at directly. It is an old and easy idea that God's light dazzles us. This could make it less surprising that the Spirit is harder to comprehend than the Father and the Son, strangely not more accessible but less; or rather, more accessible in a different way, lighting up everything else around us.

The main evidence for Christian belief in the living God is the complex testimony of the first followers of Christ to their experience before and after his resurrection. Christians trust that in the end their good news will become plain, and that everyone will eventually come to understand that the Lord they are following is the Way, the Truth, and the Life.[35] This is where Christians take their stand. The New Testament witnesses provide the data for the belief that in spite of everything God is in control, because Jesus Christ is the Son of God, who came into human history, lived, died, and rose again.

Would he have come if human beings had not sinned? It seems acceptable to suppose that the Son's coming in the fullness of time to live a human life and reveal the good news of the heavenly Father was always God's purpose. When human beings failed to welcome him, the Creator's infinite resourcefulness was not defeated. We may dare to think of Good Friday and Easter as God's awesome Plan B.

32. Gen 1:2.
33. John 20:22.
34. Acts 2:1–4.
35. John 14:6.

Part II
Belonging

10

One Another

The Pauline letters were letters from the apostle
to the churches, not letters from God to St Paul.

JAMES BARR (1972), 123

CHRISTIANS PUT THEIR TRUST in God. To put one's trust in somebody
is a responsible action, not a passive experience. A hopeful inquirer
needs to be given reasons for taking that plunge. A mystic may be able
to find God directly and trust God simply without depending upon inter-
mediaries, but most people need the testimony of one another. We rely,
explicitly or implicitly, upon the cumulative evidence of witnesses. I can
decide to put my trust in God, but I cannot decide that I will trust God to
exist.[1] What I can do is attend to the many people who have testified that
God is indeed findable, in the hope that I can belong with them.

For belief to be reasonable it needs the support of reasoning; but that
does not have to mean setting oneself doggedly to *think*, all on one's own.
Believers are not incessantly pursuing arguments. They are entering into a
tradition. Nobody has to do all the work in isolation. But that may sound
suspiciously like a vicious circle. Do we all go round and round putting the
onus of proof upon somebody else, an endless loop where nobody takes any
responsibility? Is faith as happy-go-lucky as the children's game of "pass the
parcel," which keeps going until the music stops?

1. See above, Chapter 8, heading.

Looking for a more reliable foundation, I must go back to the philosophy of my youth and take heed of the skeptical doubt about how beliefs can be well-founded.[2] In the mid-twentieth century, one was supposed to begin where Descartes began, sure of his own existence but resolved to doubt anything he could possibly doubt, even questioning his trust that other things and people existed beyond himself. To begin here made "How do you *know*?" look like the main question that students of philosophy had to address.

But the method of doubt does not turn out after all to be a good starting point for exploring the world around us. Arguing with myself keeps me closed in upon myself, out of touch with whatever else there may be. We can extricate ourselves from the trap that Descartes set, by refusing to start with the assumption that each person is all alone, but asking instead how I or anyone can find out what the real world is like. Then the parallel problem of finding out whether God is real may likewise become less intractable.

Descartes's question about whether we truly know anything would remain unanswerable for anyone who really began as a lone thinker. But isolation is nobody's real starting point. People are born into families and learn from their elders how to live in the world and explore it. Recognizing other people and communicating with them comes before, not after, finding out by experience and reasoning what kind of world we are inhabiting together.[3] Most of what we know, we have been taught. The characteristic human gift of language is no decorative garnish. Keeping in touch with one another is a basic human need and a basic human capacity. Autonomy is all very well, but interdependence is better for human creatures.[4]

My terms of reference are that I have lived all my life among other human beings, at home in the same world. I never made a discovery that other people are real like me. They brought me up to be like them. This account of how people arrive at understanding makes sense because we have seen it work in practice: not Descartes' argument, "I think, therefore I am," but the dawning awareness, "What I am is a human being."

If one followed Descartes into skeptical doubt, then it would not do to trust that any of one's assumptions answer to reality, whether about the material world, or other minds, or God. The reply to Descartes must be: there

---

2. See above, Chapter 7, 50–51; Oppenheimer, *On Being Someone*, Chapter 2, e.g., 13.

3. See Oppenheimer, *On Being Someone*, 14–15.

4. See above, Chapter 1, 10.

is no need to follow that path.[5] That is not the way anyone has to live. Rather than starting alone and fortunately finding companions, we recognize ourselves all along in a world full of people who experience events together and tell each other about what to expect. We accept that they are what they seem to be; and they turn out to be reliable enough to keep confirming that hypothesis rather than upsetting it.[6]

Responsible religious faith can take a similar route. Belief in God is more reliable if it can be a joint undertaking. I do not have to work out my own creed, but learn what other people teach me: so long as somewhere the weight of the argument is carried. The hypothesis of faith is backed by the testimony of people through the centuries to their positive experiences of encountering God. In the stained glass windows in Chartres cathedral, there are memorable images of the Evangelists sitting on the shoulders of the prophets.

At least I am certain that human beings exist. It is not faithless to find one another more evidently real than God. When a school friend of St. Augustine died, he was deeply perplexed.[7] He told himself to wait for God's help, but his soul "did not obey. And in this," said Augustine, "she was right because, to her, the well-loved man whom she had lost was better and more real than the shadowy being in whom I would have her trust."

At times when it seems that there is nothing there to back up Christian belief, only "the melancholy, long, withdrawing roar" of the ebbing tide, Matthew Arnold's "Ah, love, let us be true To one another!"[8] is a good place to stand. If I lost faith in God, faith in people would still be left. I have not lost faith in God, because I am able to trust the accumulated experience of other people. Some of them testify credibly to a direct awareness of God's presence. For the many people whose route is more indirect, deciding *who* can be trusted is just as rational as asking *what* can be proved by theoretical analysis, though less manageable by rules of logic.

This argument must not be rushed. It would be too easy to slide into saying: "Just as I believe in people because they show me, so I believe in God because God shows me." Often God does not, which is why there are far more skeptics about God than philosophical doubters about the existence of other minds. To fret that perhaps there are no other people

5. See Oppenheimer, *On Being Someone,* 19.

6. See above, Chapter 7, 47–48, Chapter 8, 59, Chapter 9, 67.

7. Augustine, *Confessions,* IV, iv, 9.

8. Matthew Arnold, "Dover Beach," *Poetical Works,* 401–2.

would be an aberration. Solipsism, "sole-self-ism," is rightly regarded as an academic exercise. Agnosticism about the existence of God has to be acknowledged as a live and honorable option, especially for people who have been confronted by indubitable evil. Most of us have to find our way with no plain sight of God's reality. We can however discern moral reasons why the Almighty would very likely be concealed, not indeed inaccessible, but elusive, in order to allow the world to provide a setting for human creatures to live and grow.

Believers trust each other before they trust God. First, people show me that a great many people exist; and then some people show me their understanding that God exists. I am not required to depend upon an argument of my own: "Since I did not make myself, therefore there must be a God who made me: QED." Knowledge of God is cumulative.[9] When Isaiah "saw the Lord high and lifted up,"[10] he was in the Temple where God was already worshiped, not arguing with himself like Descartes. Isaiah's vision incorporated him into an existing tradition, to which in turn he added his inspired contribution.

More audaciously, Christians can take to heart the New Testament understanding that Christ himself, the perfect man, needed to have the experience of being taught by other people. It is not perplexing that as a child he learnt from his mother; nor that at twelve years old he asked questions of the doctors in the Temple;[11] nor that according to the Epistle to the Hebrews he "learnt obedience through what he suffered."[12] The story of the Syro-Phoenician woman who argued with Jesus about whether he would heal her daughter, and won the argument,[13] looks harder to fit into the Christian conviction that Jesus was divine and knew best all the time. This narrative becomes positively encouraging if it is allowed to illuminate what it means for God to be made man, an example of the Lord needing to find his way as a human being.

For such important lessons as where to put one's trust, showing is better than telling. Some believers live in such a way that their lives are a strong kind of witness. Other believers live in ways so cold-hearted, or so sentimental, or so muddled, that their faith looks incredible. Atheists

9. See Mitchell, *The Justification of Religious Belief*, e.g., Chapter 3.

10. Isa 6.

11. Luke 2:46.

12. Heb 5:8.

13. Matt 15:21–28; Mark 7:25–30.

see clearly how often believers go wrong, both intellectually and morally. Christians still maintain that even bad errors where we seriously mislead one another need not wreck belief in God, any more than our frequent misunderstandings of other people need make our common life an illusion. There are enough people who take up the joint enterprise of faith, who find it increasingly worthwhile, who show one another what they have found, to make it a reasonable choice to join with them in their search. Faith is, one might say, time-honored.

Christians have been glad to use the words "I know that my redeemer liveth"[14] as a good way of affirming their faith. As my own creed, I feel safer with "I believe," backed up with evidence; and the evidence is provided by the three standard kinds of authority: scripture, tradition, and reason.[15] Scripture and tradition both consist of the witness of other people. Reason is my own responsibility but not my lonely responsibility. I reason better in company. As an Anglican Christian who was brought up somewhat Protestant, I am not accustomed to talk to the saints of old, but I can gratefully believe that I owe my faith to them. I can keep in touch with some of them by reading their books.

Among the candidates for trust are the people who over many centuries found themselves inspired to write the books of the Bible. Christians believe that the scriptures communicate God's Word to them by way of human words. The people who wrote these books were real authors. The prophets and evangelists were not God's secretaries taking dictation, never allowed either to fall into any errors or to make any creative contribution.

In the twenty-first century, strangely enough, it has become more needful, not less, to beware of threateningly mechanical ways of understanding the authority of holy scripture. The attitude that sets up all the words of the Bible as God's guaranteed divine Word looks like a kind of Protestant counterpart to the more Catholic attitude that sets up the saints of the church as fit for veneration almost amounting to worship.

When readers pronounce confidently from the lectern, "This is the word of the Lord," they seem to suggest that the Bible is one book, whose author is God. Christians who are slipping into this insidious misapprehension would generally not want to be reckoned as "fundamentalists." They would hate to be doctrinaire about their own faith, or to unchurch other believers as sham Christians. But they are losing sight of the variety of God's

14. Job 19:25.
15. See above, Chapter 7, p. 50.

communications with people, and they are taking up a position which exposes their Christianity to the hostile criticisms of Richard Dawkins and the "new atheists."

The Bible begins with ancient stories that tell what God the Creator is like. So far, so good. Many loyal Christians do not feel obliged to treat these stories as literal history; and have learnt to take as inspired myths the accounts in the Book of Genesis of how the universe began. They quite understand that people can make true statements by using poetic imagery. When they assert that God is Maker of heaven and earth, they do not worry that the "days" of creation were millions of years, any more than they suppose that their God actually keeps them safe under his feathers.[16]

But suppose that sometimes the biblical writers were wrong about the facts, and the vigorous statements they make are not true but misleading? If believers can accept the idea that the scriptures are inspired, but not dictated, then they should be willing to understand that inspiration may be a matter of degree. C. F. D. Moule stated firmly that there is "no serious reason for thinking the Bible (either Testament) to be infallible."[17]

James Barr severely, indeed scornfully, criticized fundamentalists.[18] He was not accusing them, unfairly, of taking the words of the Bible too literally, deaf to its poetry. A fundamentalist Christian can use imagery, happy to describe God as the Good Shepherd, without expecting the flock to bleat like woolly sheep. Barr explains what is wrong with fundamentalism: the dogma that nothing the Bible says, whether expressed in prose or poetry, could ever be misleading. He pointed out that the very people who maintain that scripture is free from all error are actually unable to take the Bible literally. Fundamentalists turn out to be particularly likely to forsake the plain meaning, because they have to provide more far-fetched explanations of biblical statements, in order to reconcile them well enough to go on believing all of them.

The majestic recital of the creatures coming into being each day, from evening to morning,[19] tells in the form of a myth how the universe was brought into existence by God's will. There is one word in the Genesis sto-

16. Ps 91:4.

17. Moule, *Christ Alive and at Large*, 111.

18. See Barr, *Fundamentalism*, Chapter 3, e.g., 43–44, 49; *Escaping from Fundamentalism*, e.g., 96–97, 128–29; *The Bible in the Modern World*; and Dunn, *The Living Word*, especially Chapter 5.

19. Gen 1:31.

ries that is more awkward than their narrative about God's artistry: "He made the stars *also*."[20] It seems to be stated as a fact that the earth, lit by its two great lights the sun and the moon, is the center of God's creation and that the twinkling stars are a beautiful backdrop. If believers insist on reading everything the first chapters of Genesis say as physics or history, failing to understand them as a poem that conveys to human imagination the glory of God's creative power, they may find themselves fearing modern astrophysics as if it were a threat to belief.

There is a question-begging children's hymn which says, "Jesus loves me, this I know, For the Bible tells me so." Rather than taking biblical authority as simplistically as that, it makes sense to follow a longer route. We have this great *library* of stored testimony to a particular way of understanding the universe, passed on by people in successive centuries who have lived by this tradition and found it good. At least it is reasonable to attend to them hopefully and take their message seriously. Because I can believe that *what* they said conveys the truth, I can throw in my lot with them and believe *in* the God about whom they said it.

If this is the best way to understand faith, coming to believe is not much like working out a sum, sure to get the right answer if only I am careful. Nor is it at all like having an intuition and saying "I just know." It is more like considering the available data and using my reason to weigh it up. I adopt this proposed *hypothesis* and set about finding out whether I can confirm it.[21] Of course I might fail to confirm it. I cannot prove that there is a God, but surely it is in order to try out this theory, to act on the testimony that I have been offered and see how I get on.

It is better still if I can say, see how *we* get on. I am willingly entering into a tradition that has been handed on to me. Christian faith is based upon the cumulative and cooperative development of many people's belief in God.[22] The old argument from religious experience was founded on a person's own awareness: "*I* saw this, I had this experience, so I *know*." When faith is treated as a hypothesis for us to confirm together, it can rest more securely on the threefold foundation of *scripture* recorded, *tradition* communicated, and *reason* applied.[23]

---

20. Gen 1:16.

21. See note 6 above.

22. See note 9 above.

23. See above, Chapter 7, 50 and Chapter 10, 77.

The Christian church hands on the New Testament narratives of the life, death, and resurrection of Jesus Christ, which themselves rely upon the Hebrew writings that tell what had happened before Jesus was born. For people to be able to receive these scriptures as true and enter into this tradition, they need something more substantial than inspiring poetry. Unlike the creation myths in the book of Genesis, the Gospel stories, especially the proclamation of the Resurrection, must be understood as making a definite claim to be history.

Christians living in later centuries trust the testimony of the people who came before them, who had found that they could trust this particular man, who fulfilled and expanded the hopes of the tradition that they had already received. There is no need for believers to be afraid of scholars who study the Bible closely, consider the problem, set the books in their contexts, expound their meaning, and convey their message freshly to the church.[24] Indirectly but not shakily, Christians are able to believe, trust and follow the Lord Jesus, who they find reveals God to them.

24. Encouraging examples are Bauckham, *Jesus and the Eyewitnesses*; and Dunn, *Jesus Remembered* and *Beginning from Jerusalem*.

11

God in Charge

"Don't yew talk to me about Providence . . .
First he took my husband, and then he took my
'taters, but there's One Above as'll teach him to
mind his manners, if he don't look out."

DOROTHY L. SAYERS, *THE NINE TAILORS*[1]

MOST CHRISTIAN BELIEVERS WANT very much to go on believing. Christian theology is by no means morally neutral information. Statements about God have mattering built into them, because they have to do with people's hopes and fears about what will happen in their own experience. Had it turned out that the story that the universe was created by an almighty Power had no bearing on human lives, everyone but specialist scholars could have cheerfully ignored it. The hypothesis of creation could have been taken as an interesting theory about the supernatural origin and organization of the universe, a theological way of thinking about the Big Bang, fascinating indeed to some people, but academic not practical. But the Christian doctrine of creation concerns God's purposes for living creatures who mind about what happens to them and who believe that God minds about them.

When facts are value-laden, duties follow. The God depicted in the books of the Bible not only creates but commands. People who believe these narratives are obliged to pay attention to the God presented there. Anyone

1. Sayers, *The Nine Tailors*, II, first part.

who considers what it means to affirm that God is not only almighty but good and indeed *holy* can hardly say, "Yes, but never mind all that now." The faith that God is not only Maker but King and heavenly Father entails the obligation to keep in touch with God.

Christians who accept the witness of the prophets and the apostles that the Creator of the world is findable by the people who inhabit it will expect God's reality to have some effect upon the course of events. If faith means anything, the powerful God who made the universe is able to act decisively and make a noticeable difference to what happens in it. Surely the Almighty will look after his people? Believers naturally develop the conviction that their God does mighty works for them. They promptly and eagerly acknowledge the possibility, and even the likelihood, that human history will include divine miracles.

Now they need to be reminded not to move too fast. If the good news that God is in control is to carry conviction, thinking believers need to take heed of how they can responsibly affirm it. Hume's attack on the credibility of supernatural events can be answered, but may not be ignored.[2] Christians still have to remember that miraculous acts of God must, essentially, be exceptional and amazing. That is what "miracle" means: an event that is not part of the ordinary course of nature. If material things did not normally either stay put or move in predictable ways, the universe would not be a reliable habitat where people could live and grow.

When Christians try to offer a convincing account of God's active presence in human life, there is a threefold distinction that could clarify their minds.[3] First, believers characteristically expect that when they pray they will receive some elementary awareness of God's grace helping and guiding them. They do not and they should not think of themselves as puppets with God pulling the strings and controlling their behavior, but they believe that they are subjects of a King and children of a Father, who is taking notice of them, caring about them, and backing them up.

Secondly, people who put their faith in Christ have found room in their worldview for special divine acts. Extraordinary mighty works, contrary to the normal order of creation, are built in to the gospel narrative. The God who created the physical universe and who inaugurated all the processes in it can and does intervene sometimes to control what happens. Christians still need to emphasize how special such acts of God must be. If

2. See above, Chapter 9, 66.

3. I pursued this argument first in *Incarnation and Immanence*.

the Almighty often took action to override the ordinary course of nature to make things go better, there would be no dependable course of nature and human life as we know it would be impossible.

Thirdly, between daily *grace* guiding people's lives and exceptional *miracles* in history is the idea of divine *providence,* a kind of steady pressure continually regulating the material world according to God's will; and that notion has been made to bear too much weight. It needs attention, before any more can be said about how people can expect to recognize God's presence in their lives. It turns out, surprisingly, that belief in ordinary providence is harder than belief in occasional miracles. If God is our Father, surely he will look after his children? But often it appears that he does not; and we can begin to see why not.

Faithful people are apt to expect that God will graciously move natural events in a favorable direction for their sake; but such divine responses to their prayers must be more remarkable, more miraculous, than believers are inclined to suppose. If God's care for creation meant that God kept pushing physical objects about, whether violently or gently, there would be no scope for creatures to live and make choices. The earth is the habitat on whose solidity we depend. It may not be wholly self-enclosed, and perhaps it is lit from outside;[4] but if it turned out to be continually disturbed, we should have less freedom to live our lives than fish in a tank. Foreseeable providences are harder to accommodate in a coherent universe than surprising miracles. If the rain did not generally fall alike on the just and the unjust,[5] human moral life would be a sham. One aspect of God's fatherly love is the patience to allow the creation its own reality, to let it develop without tinkering with it. The human creatures whose long-term fulfillment God intends are not robots, nor cuddly toys, nor even domestic pets.

Some people think that their faith requires them to believe that every occurrence is *meant.* Everything that happens to them must have been arranged on purpose, however hateful it may seem. That simple belief does not cohere well, either with what we know about the world of nature, or with what we have been told about God. This is serious: it builds up disappointment and disillusionment. When pious people assume that all the difficulties of their lives must be God's will for them, the faith demanded of them looks more like a burden than a comfort.

4. See above, 4 (top).
5. Matt 5:45.

Does the Almighty arrange the weather? English Christians have been instructed to avow in their public prayers[6] that they have been "justly humbled" by God's "late plague of immoderate rain and waters"; but that prayer is seldom used now. Should people who live by horticulture and tourism readily infer, when no rain has fallen for weeks except on a public holiday, that their God is angry with them? Nowadays they are more likely to conclude that there is no such Being as God.

The notion that all the occurrences in our lives must be accepted as the Lord's divine plan for us is not in the Christian creeds, and is incredible. When terrible natural disasters strike, for which no human sin can be blamed, of course faith in divine providence wobbles. Is this torment really God's will? It is more heartening to remember Elijah, who realized that "the Lord was *not* in the earthquake."[7] Not everything that happens is directly part of God's purpose. The Creator of the universe takes real risks that events may go wrong, for the sake of the ultimate outcome.

It is an insult to say to people in trouble, "Accept God's will and be grateful. This is all according to plan." The comforters who are a help when something appalling has happened, like a fatal accident or a beloved baby dying, are the ones who set us free to believe that some happenings in this world are against God's will. W. H. Vanstone declared in his inspiring book *Love's Endeavour, Love's Expense* that the place to look for God's presence in creation is not at the top of a mountain, sending down an avalanche, but at the foot of the mountain, receiving its impact.[8] Instead of saying to one another and to our children, "God did it; so we must call it good," it is more convincing, and more encouraging, to say, "God knows and God minds."[9] Our foundation for believing that God will find a way to bring good out of this at last is that God's Son first went all the way through human catastrophe and then rose again from death. The encouragement that Christian faith offers for facing the problem of evil is the hope that a universe in which evil has been overcome can eventually be transformed into a more excellent world than an undemanding universe where everything has always been predictably easy.[10]

---

6. *Book of Common Prayer*, "Thanksgiving for Fair Weather."

7. 1 Kgs 19:11.

8. Vanstone, *Love's Endeavour, Love's Expense*, 64–65.

9. For the traditional belief that God is "impassible," see Oppenheimer, *On Being Someone*, 177–79.

10. See Oppenheimer, *Making Good*, Chapters 19–21, e.g., 115–16.

The basis of Christian faith is the shared belief of Christians in the one central miracle of the Resurrection: not in recurring divine interruptions to their ordinary lives. They need not confidently expect to see the providential hand of God on the steering wheel of nature. It makes more sense to believe that God launched the universe "in the beginning"; that its continued existence is upheld by God's active power; that God can and does communicate, generally unobtrusively, with human creatures; that indeed it will all come to good in the end; but still that God generally lets nature develop and history run its course without continual adjustments.

Faith which dispenses with divine interventions is called *deism*, and Christians are apt to find it frightening: surely their God cannot be an absentee landlord? They should notice that the creeds say nothing about divine providence arranging what happens in the world. When Christians affirm what they believe, they go straight from the one God the Father Almighty, Maker of heaven and earth, to Jesus Christ his only Son our Lord, who for our salvation came down from heaven. That is indeed the crucial assertion of the Christian gospel.[11]

Christians need not be afraid of going a long way with deism. They do not go the whole way, because they tell the story of the Cross. The Creator, who made the universe and lets it be, acted at one particular time by entering into human life. Jesus Christ is God present in the world.[12] That conviction, spelt out carefully in the books of the New Testament, bases Christian faith upon a God who is not an Unmoved Mover, but decisively concerned with humanity. The Christian answer to skeptics who deny that God is findable is based upon this particular set of historical events: the life, death and resurrection of Jesus the Son of God. Christians give thanks to their Creator, not necessarily for providential manifestations but distinctively for "the redemption of the world by our Lord Jesus Christ; for the means of grace and for the hope of glory."[13]

It may be objected that to cast doubt on providence and go so far with deism is to go a long way from the gospel. The Lord himself was far from being a deist. The Father he trusted was accessible and active, and responded to the Son's prayers with marvels that convinced people that this man living among them was no ordinary man. Jesus told his disciples that it was only their lack of faith that prevented them from doing mighty works as he

11. See above, Chapter 5, 36, 38, Chapter 9, 62f.

12. Matt 1:22–23.

13. "The General Thanksgiving" in *The Book of Common Prayer*.

did.[14] In the early days of the church they did indeed do wonders, which people took as evidence that they were telling the truth.[15]

The amazement is the point. If God did enter into human life, that was an event so exceptional that it might well be attended by astonishing consequences. The miracles of the gospel are not God's everyday management of the creation to keep it running efficiently. They are, so to say, particular messages, special communications of the good news that God is truly alive and perfectly good. The Almighty coming among us did not put the ordinary workings of nature into abeyance. The rain went on falling on the just and the unjust[16] and the tower of Siloam did fall down, unhappily killing eighteen people, who were not exceptionally sinful.[17]

David Hume's argument needs to be heeded that believers should not make use of miracle stories to show that there must be a God.[18] Human credulity and sensation-mongering are always more likely explanations of surprising data than divine manipulations of natural events. Without the central miracle of Christ rising from the dead, tales of wonders would even be an embarrassment to Christians trying to commend their faith to thoughtful people today. The evidence for God's reality is not magical tricks showing how powerful the Creator is. That is not how the Christian argument goes.

The gospel is rather: The evidence which Christians offer for belief in God, the Maker of the universe, is grounded is one particular account of how God acted in the world. The one miracle that matters is not an arbitrary marvel but an integral part of this narrative. The God who created the world took responsibility for it, by coming at a particular time as an individual human being, who lived and died and who rose again. Christians affirm that God is able to bring everything to good in the end, to confront the rival worldview that everything happened by chance and will come to nothing.

14. E.g., Matt 17:20; Luke 17:6.

15. Acts 3:1–10.

16. See note 5 above.

17. Luke 13:4.

18. See note 2 above.

12

Christian Hope

> He did not say, "You shall not be tormented, you
> shall not be troubled, you shall not be grieved,"
> but he said, "You shall not be overcome."
> JULIAN OF NORWICH, *REVELATIONS OF DIVINE LOVE*, CH. 68

THE CHRISTIAN STORY ABOUT the universe is that the Lord who created it has been here. Christians are not called upon to worship a God who sits on high looking down upon our struggles, but a God who knows what mortal life is like. That is the meaning, straightforward rather than abstruse, which Christians find in the life and death of Jesus, the man who was "God with us." The "Creed of St. Athanasius" states carefully that "our Lord Jesus Christ, the Son of God, is God and Man"; and that he lived and died as a human being for our sake.[1] I would dare to say that only that God has the right to make a world like this in which some creatures suffer so badly.[2]

If we can believe that God the Creator could be present on the Cross, then we can believe that God is not absent from people who are in pain, or isolated, or abused, or disabled, or frail.[3] The Maker of the universe is "acquainted with grief"[4] and knows at first hand what it is like to be aban-

1. See the "Creed of St Athanasius," in *The Book of Common Prayer*, after Morning and Evening Prayer; the "Nicene Creed," in the Communion service; also "The Thirty-nine Articles," article II, 19.

2. See Oppenheimer, *Making Good*, e.g., 45.

3. See "God impassible?" under "God", in the Index.

4. Isa 53:3.

doned and afraid, even to be afraid of death.[5] The Son of God was forsaken by his friends[6] and felt himself to be forsaken by his Father.[7]

Christians used to swear, often unthinkingly, "Zounds"—God's wounds. To consider God's human dismay should be still more awesome. Of all the Gospel stories, Gethsemane and the cry of desolation are assuredly fact not legend. They are not tales that disciples would make up to impress gullible inquirers. Because Christians can believe these accounts of the Passion, the suffering, of the Son of God, they can stop supposing whatever happens that they must always say "never mind," gratefully welcoming the troubles of their lives, confident that God is up there arranging everything, including their woes. What they can say in dire distress is that God is on their side and that God is finally in charge.

It can be painfully hard to look hopefully at the creation. If Christians maintain that all is well already, no wonder there are so many unbelievers. The problem of evil is more weighty than that. Some aspects of human experience are severe challenges to faith, for all the serenity some wise people develop. For faith in God's justice to stand up, the Christian hope that all shall be well at last needs not just assertion but vindication. Good Friday without Easter Sunday would be a tragic narrative of dedicated heroism: a disaster not a victory. The accounts of the crucifixion are only too easy to believe; but if the story had ended so, the message would hardly have been worth passing on for two thousand years.

The Cross is not the end of the story; but the point of the story. When Jesus prayed humanly and divinely, "Not my will but thine,"[8] he accepted that for him this was going to mean pain and death. The bitter cup had to be drunk. Christians ever since have been inclined to suppose that God's purpose must always be the outcome that they do not want. "God's will be done," they say, with resignation at best, sometimes with bitterness. But the suffering that the Lord faced on the Friday we call Good, although foreseen, permitted, and chosen, was not itself the will of God at all. It was on the third day that the Father truly answered the prayer in Gethsemane. God's will was indeed done when the Son rose from the dead.

That God in Christ went through death and overcame death is the keystone that holds together the structure of Christian faith, allowing God's

5. Matt 26:37–45; Mark 14:33–41; Luke 22:41–45.

6. Matt 26:56; Mark 14:50.

7. Matt 28:46; Mark 15:34; Ps 22:1.

8. Matt 26:39; Mark 14:36; Luke 22:42.

creation to be called good.[9] Good Friday and Easter Sunday together support the hypothesis that in the end God can and will bring the universe to excellence. The rising of Christ is the pledge that whatever tribulations beset God's creatures, from childish afflictions to the sad diminishments of old age, will turn out in the end to be compatible with the Creator's purposes. Somehow good shall come from them, enough good to make the troubles worthwhile.

But here arises the difficulty that is known as "the scandal of particularity." Can the human sufferings of Jesus Christ really represent *all* kinds of trouble, so that people can always tell each other, "The Lord has been here, in this predicament we are in now"? In living a real human life, Jesus could not experience at first hand every possible ordeal that human beings undergo. Because he was cut off in his prime, how can he be alongside people in old age? Peter Coleman called his Leveson lecture "Is Christianity the Friend of Ageing?" He pointed out that "Christianity of all the great religions gives apparently little significance to ageing. Partly," he explained, "this is because Christ died in early adulthood at an age that came to be seen as the perfect age . . ."[10]

Women may particularly feel this difficulty. They have been told all along that Christ is the perfect *man*. Until recently they have been forbidden to consider themselves as the sort of human being who can represent Christ. As they get older, they may wonder how Christ can be the sort of human being whose trials can represent their trials, since the Lord never had to cope with the mortifications of having become an old woman. The answer to that objection must be that Christ's Passion can stand for every human ill without actually exemplifying every particular human ill. Can we think of any woes of men and women which cannot find their counterpart in the terror, savagery, pain, grief, loneliness, and injustice of the Cross? The Lord never grew old; but people who have found growing old a bad experience may find their troubles truly represented by his physical weakness and pain; by the closing down of the satisfying activities of life; and especially by the inexorable loss of control. The death of Jesus was not the plain triumph of a confident martyr, but shared the helplessness of many who suffer without any assurance that all will be well.

This reasoning is not intended as a sermon. It is meant to be an argument about the problem of evil, as it presents itself to people who can see

9. Gen 1:31.

10. Coleman, "Is Christianity the Friend of Ageing?," 18.

that human lives often do not arrive at happy endings and who want to know whether the Christian story has real encouragement to offer. I am contending that if we acknowledge honestly how hard the loss of youthful hope can be, we can still understand that faith in God is not refuted, either by troubles of one's own, or by concern for other people's suffering. When people are unhappy at the fragility of human life, and when they are distressed by the negative ways they or their fellow human beings are experiencing the passing of time, the Cross of Christ offers them God's company in their trials and the Resurrection of Christ offers them assurance of God's victory over catastrophe.

Of these, the idea that God is present is the easier. The idea that God is triumphant is harder to make one's own. People who are not already disposed to believe will pick out the gaps in the argument. For critical skeptics, the biggest gap is likely to be what believers take as the biggest encouragement: the persistent hope that the troubles of this world will be made good in heaven. The notion of eternal life, gathering up the broken fragments of human existence and setting everything to rights at last, cannot be an optional extra for people who believe in a good God. "You *must* have faith" will not do; but Christians maintain, "You *can* have faith." If I did not find it credible that Christ rose from death, "the first-fruits of them that slept,"[11] I could not call myself a Christian.[12]

Much depends upon the notion of life renewed. Seemingly rational human beings down the centuries have found the concept of *regeneration* illuminating. The New Testament analogy of the seed that is buried, so that the new plant can grow, encourages the idea that death may indeed be followed by new life and that dying may even be a condition making new life possible.

The normal rhythms of life, being born, maturing, letting go, are a foundation not only for human comfort but for good theology. "Those who want to save their life will lose it."[13] A grain of wheat has to fall into the ground and die to produce a harvest.[14] That is a hopeful image for the Christian hope for life restored by way of death. Of course analogies must not be pressed too hard. Seeds do not perish distressingly as some human

11. 1 Cor 15:20.

12. I tried to fill out the idea of resurrection somewhat in Oppenheimer, *The Hope of Heaven*.

13. Matt 16:25; Mark 8:35; Luke 9:24; and John 12:24.

14. John 12:25.

beings do. The problem of evil remains; but the universal processes of aging and mortality need not, in themselves, be at the heart of it, as if they settled the argument against the goodness of God.

When we think about what heavenly life might be like, a certain agnosticism must be appropriate. It is unwise to set about specifying, with audacious confidence, the conditions of a world where we shall all be young and strong and healthy, and all tears will be wiped away from our eyes. The fact that we cannot imagine it does not make it nonsense. Attempts to describe the kingdom of heaven to one another may be compared with the way children play at being grown-up, without having much idea yet what adult life will be like. We may be blessed with insights, provided that we keep our minds open to the idea that we have a lot to learn.

Faith in God through Christ would remain incomplete, if the good news of the Lord's Resurrection did not apply to the hopes believers cherish, for themselves and the particular people they love, that their present experience is not the whole story. "The last enemy to be destroyed is death."[15] St. Paul called the prospect of a new life with no more dying a mystery.[16] It is indeed, because we cannot see beyond the horizon of this world, where we are still swimming like goldfish who cannot see out.

The definite claim Christians make is that Christ the Lord is there already and has prepared a place for them.[17] They have reasons to give for believing that claim. They may continue to be beset by questions about whether their eternal hopes really have any substance. Academic arguments starting from premises and leading to conclusions may carry more or less intellectual conviction; but if people are to live by the answers their arguments reach, they must find out how to express their theoretical notions in terms of their own experience. They can use assorted images to explore what transcendence might mean.

Thomas Traherne was not the only child to see the reflections in a puddle as an image of another world, which he could see "through a little watery chink which some dry ox or horse might drink . . ."[18] Less fancifully, many have used the making of music as a way of taking hold of a kind of reality beyond ordinary experience. Browning suggested that "out of three

15. 1 Cor 15:26.
16. 1 Cor 15:51.
17. John 14:2.
18. Traherne, "Shadows in the Water." See above, Chapter 1, 3.

sounds" someone can "frame, Not a fourth sound, but a star."[19] To use images like this is not to make poetry a substitute for fact, but to use poetic awareness to illuminate how transcendence might be real.

Agnosticism must be appropriate about what heaven may be like, but followers of Christ have confidence that heaven is a credible destination, a matter of fact not fantasy. There is no need to try to specify the physics of the next world, nor the biology of celestial beings, especially as the physics of the universe we are inhabiting now is already beyond plain comprehension.[20] Without attempting to establish any one picture as compulsory, Christians can try to shed light from different directions upon the truth they glimpse.

On the one hand, they can leave aside legalistic fears that the only appropriate image for the next world is a divine law-court meting out stern impersonal justice. On the other hand, they need not be committed to the sentimentality of the *in memoriam* notices in the local paper, which announce that another little angel has arrived up there. It is more promising to consider what teaching the Bible does offer about everlasting life. If a framework can be put in place, there need not be pressure to fill in the details forthwith. The information that the Gospels provide is not about divine science but about the ethics of God's kingdom, the way of life for which human beings are made.

To envisage existence in a heavenly world, we can extrapolate from what we understand already about how human beings are meant to live. Trusting the promise that "God shall be all in all"[21] need not mean crediting the alarming notion that eventually each of us will outgrow our minding about one another in order to love God alone. Heaven is not to be imagined as a destination for immortal souls in isolation from one another. It would, literally, be hell to be banished from community and imprisoned in oneself. The worship for which God's people are created is indeed to be single-minded rather than distracted, but human beings are not made to be solitary rather than sociable.

The Lord's second great commandment, "Thou shalt love thy neighbor as thyself"[22] is surely no "interim ethic" valid only for present conditions and due to be superseded by the vision of God. If that commandment is

19. Browning, "Abt Vogler," *Poems*, vol. 1, 777–781.

20. See Oppenheimer, *Making Good*, 137.

21. 1 Cor 15:28.

22. Matt 22:39.

to be obeyed and come into its own in the kingdom of heaven, our living among other people and making a difference to one another's happiness cannot be a temporary arrangement. We should think of our interdependence as having eternal validity.[23]

Pious people shy away from specifying selfishly what comfort or reward they wish for themselves, but they might reach more reliable ideas of what their Christian hope might mean, by considering what they would wish for each other. Just as Christians develop their everyday faith in company, so they can best picture eternal fulfilment as something which people are supposed to find and enjoy together. "I believe in the Communion of Saints" is not a childish fancy but a clause in the creed. We can use imagery to fashion some positive ideas, naive but not foolish, about a world where heavenly hopes of human flourishing would come true.

The kingdom of heaven is a promise, not a threat. In the Gospels, two images stand out. A characteristic recurring picture is God's welcome at a feast of celebration.[24] It is not a prospect of an endless rota of solemn divine service, but an invitation to take a place made ready, at a gathering to be enjoyed in good company.

Admission to the heavenly celebration is not exactly unconditional. What is necessary for enabling anyone to enter God's kingdom is expressed in a different image which also is positive: one must be born again.[25] An application of this basic teaching of Christ might be that the heavenly life includes being wanted, welcomed, loved, and cherished.[26] Our future destiny as children of God is not a prospect of being tormented as sinful but of being brought up as immature. Babies do not arrive in the world either burdened with shame for sins committed, or garlanded with deserving achievements, but bearing unlimited promise. James Dunn points out that St. Paul's gospel was not so much about backward-looking repentance and forgiveness as about forward-looking faith, not tasks set, but the gift of the Spirit promised.[27] "For the perfection of human nature consists perhaps in its very growth in goodness," said St. Gregory of Nyssa.[28]

---

23. See above, Chapter 1, 10 and Chapter 10, 74.

24. E.g., Matt 9:10, 22:9–10, 25:1; Luke 5:29, 7:34, 15:23; John 2:7–10.

25. John 3:3.

26. See Oppenheimer, *The Hope of Heaven*, 134–35.

27. Dunn, *Beginning from Jerusalem*, 584.

28. Gregory of Nyssa, *The Life of Moses*, prologue 10.

The image of rebirth is by no means a sentimental or a self-indulgent image. The life of a new person is not all cuddles. "You must be born again" includes the thought that the beginning of human life is not without ordeals: birth itself, weaning, and schooling.[29] The upbringing we need may be long and slow and may require a great deal of patience; but we may imagine it as a program, not a sentence.

The promise of a heavenly fresh start should not be presumed to imply that the moral and immoral lives people have led on earth count for nothing at all. Wrongs cry out to be made good, not obliterated. Sinners cannot expect to enter self-confidently into the new life without facing the damage we have done and being given the opportunity to make peace with the victims we have hurt. More hopefully, human beings who have grown to be saints will surely be encouraged to thank other people and celebrate the blessings they owe to them. Instead of finding resentfully that "hell is other people,"[30] we might be permitted to take up the notion of purgatory and imagine it as an antechamber to heaven, a place for meeting one another, discovering or rediscovering what we have in common. Christian hope might revise the last verse of Psalm 86: "Show some token upon me for good, that those who *love* me may see it and be *glad*."

---

29. 1 Cor 3:1–2; Eph 4:13–15; 1 Pet 2:2; Heb 5:12–14. See Oppenheimer, *Making Good*, 172, on the image of "mother" for God and letting go.

30. Sartre, *Huis Clos*, scene 5.

13

Is Anyone There?

> So too let him rejoice and delight at finding you
> who are beyond discovery rather than fail to find
> you by supposing you to be discoverable.
>
> ST AUGUSTINE, *CONFESSIONS*, I 6

CHRISTIAN BELIEF IS HARD, because people can see for themselves that there is a great deal wrong with this world that they are told is God's creation. The gospel, the good news, takes heed of the troubles and offers reasons for believing that God is in control after all. Christian affirm that the hypothesis of God's reality is solidly founded upon experience. They take up their position on the New Testament evidence which convinces them that God was revealed in the life, death, and resurrection of Christ.[1]

The purpose of occupying a stronghold is not to keep making defensive forays against enemies but to inhabit it safely. Believers under attack are glad to be well armed with arguments, but the point of their faith is not to argue but to discover God's reality. Because they affirm that God did act at a particular time, they can sit light to the idea of finding God revealed repeatedly by conspicuous interventions in the ordinary world around them.[2]

---

1. Parts of this chapter go back to lectures given in Wells Cathedral and at St. George's House, Windsor (see Preface); and this whole line of thought goes back to a book I wrote long ago: Oppenheimer, *Incarnation and Immanence*, in which I recommended a view I called "Incarnational deism." See above, Chapter 11, 85.

2. See above, Chapter 9, 66–7; Chapter 11, 82–3, 86.

To sustain their belief in God, they do not need contemporary miracles, but they do depend upon some awareness that divine *grace* really is accompanying them in everyday life. Rather than assuming that God will supernaturally control events by putting pressure on things, they expect that God will bless people, by communicating with them in something like the ways people bless one another, by keeping in touch. They cannot often say, "God did this" or "God arranged all this for us" but they sometimes make a definite claim and say, "God is present here." Theories about God the Creator, even backed up by telling arguments, would remain vacantly theoretical without any direct encounters. Christians need some positive encouragement, not an utter blank. They hope that "times of refreshing may come from the presence of the Lord."[3]

How can people today find God's presence, once they are too sophisticated to hope for someone like Zeus or Hermes[4] to arrive and have conversations with them? They must not make irresponsible assumptions about how God is sure to act; they need not claim vainly to see beyond the bounds of the natural world; but they can keep asking themselves and one another what they do find.

For one this-worldly Christian who tries to be honest, the answer is not an empty negative but takes shape as hints and hopes.[5] I believe that without escaping from the fish tank we can see light coming in from outside. We can take part with believers through the centuries who have claimed to recognize the Spirit of the risen Christ, no longer walking about in Galilee but all over the place; or rather, wherever they go. His followers have not been left comfortless, always needing to find excuses for his current absence.[6] They cannot produce knock-down proofs, they have no hot line to heaven, most of them are not mystics; but they realize, often with hindsight, that his unobtrusive presence has been there all along.

If such hopeful ideas are to provide a solid support for faith, they must be made more definite. Christians affirm that God is findable. Their Bible, their tradition, and sometimes their own awareness, offer them the hypothesis, which many reasonable human beings find credible, of a Power present in human life, who is to be imagined as a Person, or, more technically, as three Persons in one God. They look for God's presence, and they believe

---

3. Acts 3:19, quoting Isa 3:19.

4. Acts 15:11–12.

5. See Oppenheimer, *Incarnation and Immanence,* 52–54, 59f.

6. John 14:18.

that they do discover it revealed in scripture, tradition, and reason,[7] in their best ideas and feelings, in their moral consciences, in the immensity and intricacy of the natural world, in human kindness,[8] and particularly in the breaking of bread.[9]

Faith in God is promisingly based upon narratives about Someone who is active and accessible, not inert or remote. From the beginning of the Bible, God's creating the universe and God's communicating with the human creatures who live in it are developments of the same story. The Book of Genesis introduces God, not first as King or Judge nor even as Father, but as Speaker. It was God's Word that brought order out of chaos. "*In the beginning* God created the heavens and the earth . . . And *God said*, 'Let there be light'; and there was light."[10] The first verse of the Fourth Gospel picks up the first verses of Genesis: "*In the beginning* was the *Word*." It is hard to understand how the translators of the New English Bible could ignore this echo, happily restored in the Revised English Bible.

Of course the description of God the Creator as Speaker is picture-language. "God said" is not a statement about vocal cords. The Word of God is God's means of communication with creatures. It is the way God is made known, whatever that is turning out to be. The Fourth Gospel immediately identifies God's Word in the beginning, which called the world into existence, with Jesus the Son of God, who came into the world to make God known to humanity.[11]

To recognize a particular human person as God speaking to human beings is a kind of transcendent mixed metaphor come true. A problem for translators is that the Greek "logos," which means "word," also means "reason"; and English can convey only one of these at a time. We have to switch to and fro between calling Jesus God's Word and God's Reason personified. However profound a meaning we are able to give to *the Logos*, the central message is that Jesus of Nazareth expresses in human life the rational speech of the Creator, through whom all things came into being. The message is stated more simply in Matthew's nativity story, that Jesus Christ is *God with us*[12] in human form.

7. See above, Chapter 7, 50, Chapter 10, 77, 80.

8. See, e.g., Matt 25:40.

9. See Oppenheimer, *Helping Children Find God*, Chapters 16 and 17.

10. Gen 1: 2–3.

11. John 1:1 and 14

12. Matt 1:22–23.

The Epistle to the Hebrews likewise connects the idea of God who speaks with the idea of God who makes. "God spoke to our ancestors in many and various ways" and at last "he has spoken to us by a Son."[13] The Son, by whom God communicates with human beings, is identified as the "heir of all things, through whom he also created the worlds."[14] The word "Logos" is not used here, let alone personified as Someone: but still God is both Speaker and Maker.

The Epistle to the Hebrews goes on to develop sophisticated theological descriptions of God the Son.[15] He is the reflection of God's glory; "the exact imprint of God's very being"; "he sustains all things by his powerful word." All the images are evidently picture-language. Maybe, from God's point of view, all these ways of speaking about God's dealings with the creation are as childish as the primitive mythology of Genesis chapter 3, where the Lord God walked in the garden in the cool of the day, hoping to enjoy the company of his human creatures.

As the story goes on in Genesis, God calls to Adam, "Where are you?"[16] But Adam has sinned and is hiding among the leaves. Communication between people and their Maker is impaired. This fact is too clear, whatever myth or history we invoke to account for it. Yet the whole biblical saga of God's people assumes that communication is not destroyed. There has always been the conviction that God is sometimes heard addressing chosen individuals in words, saying things like, "Whom shall I send, and who will go for us?"[17]

For people to be able to keep in touch with their Maker, people must be enough like God to be able to interact. The most distinctive fact about humanity is that we are language-users.[18] The skill of speaking to one another is the most ambitious lesson new human beings have to learn, surely a lesson preparing them for heavenly as well as for earthly life. It makes sense to locate the image of God first of all in our speech. Christians want to get to the moral point at once and talk about divine and human *love* as fundamental: but to be capable of loving, people must first be capable of communicating.

13. Heb 1:1–2.

14. Ibid.

15. Heb 1:3.

16. Gen 3:8.

17. Isa 6.

18. See above, Chapter 2, 16; Chapter 10, 74.

People use words to talk to God. They say things like: "Speak, Lord, for thy servant hears";[19] or even, "My God, my God, why hast thou forsaken me?"[20] For Christians, that Psalmist's desperate human appeal has been picked up in the strange disclosure, foretold but still unexpected, when in due time God's Word was made flesh and lived and died among us, and the cry of abandonment became God's own. Christians ever since can dare to claim for themselves the glimpse of hope that appears at the end of the same Psalm. God is not absent from human beings after all, because the church of Christ is "a people that shall be born, whom the Lord hath made."

The encouraging hints and hopes[21] of God's presence cannot all be reserved for other people. Sooner or later, in order to be a follower of Christ, I must consider where I can find my place in the story Christians tell. How can *I*, not only the prophets of old or the chosen apostles, actually keep in touch with the God who is Creator and Redeemer? As a twenty-first century Christian, I seem to be three people in different frames of mind: a beloved child; a pupil who is not alone, who is learning in the company of other learners; but often a puzzled inquirer.

It is all very well to say to myself, "Be patient" and "Listen"; but when people listen they usually expect to hear something. Human parents do talk to their children, but God generally does not.[22] Schools have timetables and the teachers are there to give lessons, before they set the homework. People who believe in Christ and are trying to follow the Christian way are bewildered, or even baffled, when these images that they took for signposts seem to lead them into dead ends. They would gladly live as docile children and obedient pupils; but they cannot avoid the obligation to explore the world around them as questioning thinkers.

Beginners looking for encouragement may be dismayed to find that even God's Son, who became a human being in order to show God to us, does not seem to be as easily accessible as their elders have led them to think. The straightforward idea of prayer as conversation with Jesus appears to be a hindrance rather than a help. The more they try, the less they feel that there is anybody there. If there is any conversation going on at all, it is more like a conversation with Satan, spun out of natural human notions, sometimes judgmental, sometimes flattering, always deceptive. "You

19. 1 Sam 3: 9–10.

20. Psalm 22; Matthew 27:46; Mark 15:34.

21. See above, 96n5.

22. See above, chapter 10, 75.

haven't a hope: real Christians pray better than this"; "How like you to do something so kind"; "You've slaved away for hours and it's time you had a little reward"; "That can wait"; "You can never tell if they really want you to come too"; "A good God would never let this happen"; "God isn't listening"; "It's just childish to imagine a God up there."

One young Christian who found a way through this kind of impasse was Austin Farrer.[23] He hoped that God would talk to him, but no voice came. Many people have given up for good at that point. Austin Farrer got rid of his frustration, not by persistently trying to keep a face-to face conversation going, but by starting somewhere different. He considered how he found God's presence inspiring his thinking from within, especially when he tried to think about God. He explained this with an analogy: "I would dare to hope that sometimes my thought would become diaphanous, so that there should be some perception of the divine cause shining through the created effect, as a deep pool, settling into a clear tranquility, permits us to see the spring in the bottom of it from which its waters rise."[24] If that sounds difficult and academic, the idea has been expressed simply in the words of a favorite prayer, "God be in my head and in my understanding."[25]

The notion of God's Spirit present within us is thoroughly characteristic of the New Testament, and more realistic than the idea of Jesus appearing to people today face to face and telling them what to do. It might sound simpler to tell beginners that praying is talking to Jesus, but the image of the Spirit praying within us is more promising for Christians who feel out of touch. Christians are not to put words into God's mouth, but they can hope, and indeed pray, that God will put ideas into their heads and words into their mouths.

Christian prayer is traditionally described as addressed *to* the Father, *through* rather than *to* the Son, *in* the Holy Spirit. For St. Paul, it is the Spirit who, indeed, in*spires* us to address God as "Our Father." "When we cry, 'Abba, Father!' it is the Spirit himself bearing witness with our spirit that we are children of God . . . Likewise the Spirit helps us in our weakness; for we do not know how to pray as we ought, but the Spirit himself intercedes for us with sighs too deep for words."[26] The reason why the Lord's Prayer

---

23. Farrer, *The Glass of Vision*. See Oppenheimer, *Helping Children Find God*, Chapter 9, especially 77; and *On Being Someone*, 146–47.

24. Farrer, *The Glass of Vision*, 7–8.

25. An early medieval prayer.

26. Rom 8:15–16, 26.

is so important to Christians is that they believe that when they use these words they are both following the teaching he gave and joining in with his disciples through the centuries.

St. Paul's correspondents were not learned people, but they found inspiration in his theological letters, treasured them and handed them on to the following generations. He expected them to have some idea of what he meant by the notion of the presence of Christ within them, "the hope of glory."[27] Likewise the readers of the First Epistle of John passed on the blunt statement, "No man has ever seen God; if we love one another, God abides in us."[28] If Christians take heed of this New Testament teaching, they may be less tempted to fob learners off with unsatisfying ideas that communicating with God must be just like a straightforward conversation with another human being, ideas that they may need painfully to unlearn. It matters that what beginners are taught should leave space for growing.

When Christians feel like losing heart because praying to God seems like trying to attract the attention of an invisible Father in heaven who is not listening, they need not succumb to permanent childishness and ignorance, but seize on to the livelier hope that they are to grow out of their inexperience. We are all to come "to maturity, to the measure of the full stature of Christ."[29] Beloved children and older questioning thinkers can hope to arrive at understanding by becoming learners, which is what "disciples" means.

Critics are too apt to imagine that the faith of Christians is juvenile dependence upon an imaginary Daddy-figure looking after them. It is no wonder that Christian moral teaching is shrunk to the kind of paternalism that hinders people's growth. But the role of a parent is to support the children's development into adult sons and daughters. Christians need not remain as helpless babies, any more than they have to be stuck in the frame of mind of schoolchildren nor even of philosophy students with set problems to discuss.

Instead of giving up in discouragement because divine inspiration fails to arrive on demand like a bolt from the blue, followers of Christ might apply his teaching about the heavenly Father by asking practical questions about the upbringing of God's children. How are the family being fed and sustained? Attending to the Bible and receiving the sacraments, rather than

27. E.g., Col 1:27.
28. 1 John 4:12.
29. Eph 4:13.

heavenly visitations, are the ordinary resources by which Christians characteristically keep in touch.

St. Augustine did receive the Word of God as a biblical bolt from the blue. He heard a voice saying "Tolle, lege," "Take up and read," and found a special message for himself straight away.[30] More often it takes years of steadily reading the scriptures, and attending to one another's experience, to accumulate stores of accessible nourishment. For a Christian looking for the inspiration of the Holy Spirit, this slower and less dramatic progress is more promising than conspicuous manifestations: not often "Eureka!" but "Yes, I begin to see." St. Paul understood that babies begin with milk and progress to solid food.[31] Christians apply the image of the heavenly Father practically, when they ask their God to keep inspiring them, not so much by giving them instructions as by showing them things, clarifying and enlightening their minds, to help them to find out about the world.

At any age, people are likely to learn best alongside other people. They can become more mature without setting off on their own. Just as separate individuals go on needing one another for their earthly physical and emotional nourishment, so they go on needing one another for divine nourishment. *I* need to keep in touch with *us*. I do not have to rely upon spiritual maturity of my own in order to qualify as a member of the family of God. I can be educated by the Bible, because the church has been given these books and has handed them down. I can be literally nourished at the sacrament of the Eucharist, when Christians meet to break bread together, to receive and share the Body of Christ, the material means of grace by which he still becomes findable on earth. I can ask other people what they think and find out what has encouraged them.

---

30. Augustine, *Confessions*, VIII, xii, 29.

31. E.g., 1 Cor 3:4.

14

The Means of Grace

> If anyone be in despair . . . let him go joyfully to
> the Sacrament . . . and seek help from the entire
> company of the spiritual body and say, "I have
> on my side Christ's righteousness, life and suffer-
> ings with all the holy angels and all the blessed in
> heaven and all good men upon earth. If I die I am
> not alone in death. If I suffer, they suffer with me."
> MARTIN LUTHER, "ON THE BLESSED SACRAMENT"

WHEN SOMEONE IS BEGINNING to follow Christ, joining the body
of Christian people is not just another step that may probably
follow after first affirming Christian belief. The Christian faith has always
been rooted in Christian community. Human beings by nature are social
creatures[1] and this applies to their piety as well as to their morality. Church
membership is more than a helpful extra. If the cliché is true that Christianity is "caught rather than taught," demonstrated rather than proved, each
Christian is knowingly or unknowingly providing data to back up or cast
doubt on the truth of the gospel. The statements that make up the creeds
include belief in the "holy catholic church" and "the Communion of Saints."
Prayer is seldom "the flight of the alone to the Alone."[2] People pray to God

1. See above, Chapter 10, 74–5.

2. Plotinus (c. 205–70), *Enneads*, VI, 9, ix. See Oppenheimer, *Helping Children Find
God*, 121.

with one another and for one another. Often they are grateful to identify themselves with other people's words and offer them to God, and sometimes they provide words for other people to use.

The church in the twenty-first century declares itself to be somehow the same body, the Body of Christ, whose cherishing was St. Paul's life work. A Christian physicist, writing to a godson who was being confirmed, did a calculation: how many people would be included in the sequence, as he put it, of "hands to heads," from a first generation bishop's hands to a twentieth century candidate's head? He worked out that there would be few enough people to gather in one room. That is a notion that enlivens the meaning of "the Communion of Saints."

There is no need to insist on pressing the question whether somebody can be a Christian outside the church. The Gospel stories about Jesus meeting people make fretful arguments about who does and who does not belong look sadly legalistic. His teaching is as exacting as any rigorist could wish, but it has a different feel, a different *spirit*, from the kind of rules some Christians want to make in his name. Must Christian disciples give such priority to correct religious observance that the children Jesus blessed one day in Galilee[3] could turn out to belong less surely to his people than the converts the apostles admitted with proper ceremonies? What special dispensation might be needed, to enable the small person whom he set in the midst and designated as the greatest in the kingdom of heaven[4] to be duly counted as an honorary member of the church? Did the bridegroom and bride, whose wedding at Cana the Lord adorned with his presence,[5] enter forthwith, unbaptized, into a valid Christian marriage?

The optional/compulsory distinction is overworked. "You must belong" and "No need to belong" fall into the same trap. Rather than propounding a law, "Church membership is compulsory for disciples," what matters is to make a statement of fact, "For people trying to find God, the church is available." Some loyal Christians risk suggesting the contrary, that seekers may not find the church available after all, because membership is reserved for conformists. The reason why the church is there is not to provide an answer to the question, "How can we decide whether somebody belongs to Christ?" What the church offers is an answer to the question, "Where can people become aware of God's reality?"

3. Matt 19:4; Mark 10:14; Luke 18:16.

4. Matt 18:1–4; Mark 9:33–37.

5. John 2:1–11.

Christians who do not claim to have everyday conversations with God, and cannot confidently identify the workings of providence in their daily lives, need, all the more, to be able to identify where they can expect to discover God. They need the findable reality of the church, if they are not to be left to their own inadequate devices. It follows that, just because they are making no claims to any conspicuous special status, they have a particular responsibility to do their best to keep in touch, for their own encouragement and for the sake of the other people who are depending upon them. Today, when many of the younger generations "have issues with" organized religion as intolerant or irrelevant, and are hardly seeking for God at all, the older ones cannot effectively encourage them with vaguely spiritual goodwill, without any particular connection with the Body where their predecessors have identified the presence of God.

Keeping in *touch* is a metaphor, but no less real for that. Of course the Christian church, the Body of Christ, is spiritual, but it is also literally tangible. The human beings who are members of Christ are physical creatures, living and acting in the material world. It is fitting for people who believe that God came to earth as an embodied human being to be literal-minded, down-to-earth, about what keeping in touch with God means. Christianity therefore is characteristically a faith that is grounded in sacraments: that is, a faith that uses physical signs to convey spiritual meaning.[6]

A sacrament is "an outward and visible sign of an inward and spiritual grace."[7] Human creatures are naturally capable of understanding that one thing can signify another. In their lives together they endow matter with meaning. They take material things and formally or informally they bless them, so that these things do indeed become human sacraments, means of human grace. Gifts convey affection, more valuable than their cash price. Wedding rings mean that these two people are joined in marriage. For mourning a beloved person, putting flowers on an honored grave has comforting significance. When families gather for a midwinter holiday, the Christmas pudding expresses festivity and celebration. People may not even find it particularly delicious, but it matters that everyone there should be offered some. A birthday present wrapped up, whether for a toddler or an octogenarian, is a serious tribute to an important person on an important day. A child too young to understand explanations of what "ritual"

---

6. I set out these ideas about the Eucharist in Oppenheimer, *Helping Children Find God*, Chapters 16 and 17

7. *The Book of Common Prayer*, "The Catechism."

means can solemnly take a deep breath to blow out the three candles on the birthday cake before it is cut into slices and eaten.

The word "sacrament" is a technical term that may look like the pious terminology of an in-group. But the people who most need material ways of giving substance to their faith may not be the ones who are able to use religious language easily, who take part in divine worship naturally, untroubled by perplexing uncertainty. It is worriers and doubters who particularly need access to the means of grace provided for them in God's name by their companions on the human journey. Depending upon the company and support of one another is more responsibly human, and less risky, than setting off independently. The pity is that reverence sometimes gives the impression that what matters more than including everyone is to protect holy rituals from unworthy approaches.

The sacrament that is provided as the ordinary way of making somebody a member of the Christian church is baptism. The water, whether sprinkled drops or total immersion, is a plain symbol for washing away the past so as to make a fresh start. The church has understood well that this rite must be accessible, and has allowed it to be administered by lay people, without quibbling here about the validity of priestly orders. Members of separated churches are at least fellow Christians, because they have their baptism in common. Christians who are horribly at odds about the boundaries of God's grace are not obliged to repudiate one another at the threshold. A follower of Christ can stand on this firm basis, without engaging in legal wrangles about eligibility, or moral arguments about who is worthy or unworthy.

Baptism is a gate for letting people in, not a barrier for shutting people out. If the Gospels are reliable at all, they teach both that God's promises can be trusted, and that God's mercy is not limited by human regulations. God can and often does bypass the proper channels.[8] Heaven forbid that people who for all manner of reasons have not found the authorized way in to the church should be repudiated in Christ's name. Believers should rather be grateful for the agreement there already is, even among argumentative legalists, that this known ritual is indeed available for offering a positive welcome to new members.

The sacrament that is available for keeping disciples in touch with their God is the Eucharist, the Thanksgiving. It has many names and many meanings; but first of all it is a meal. Sophisticated and unsophisticated

8. E.g., John 10:16.

Christians can take hold of the plain image of ordinary nourishment, to keep their faith grounded in reality. People look after each other by feeding one another; and they mark the great occasions of human life by feasting. Likewise to set about seeking God's presence by way of eating and drinking together is not frivolous nor materialistic, but profoundly fitting.

There are ways of thinking about the Eucharist that though time-honored are less helpful for building up faith. For some Christians, it appears that this sacrament is all about death. Whether they have been taught that the Eucharist is the sacrifice of a victim, or whether they consider it as no more than a memorial service, its meaning seems gloomy and frightening. They seem to suggest that eating the bread must mean horribly eating the dead body of Christ, or anyway concentrating on his dying, rather than on being nourished in his company.

If they take up a way of thinking that is just as traditional and no less reverent, and call the Eucharist the Lord's Supper, they can first put the meal in the upper room in context by realizing that the Lord did not have supper only once. It is important to tell beginners that Jesus ate and drank with his friends, both on ordinary days and on special occasions. The idea that the Eucharist is a image of how God gives life by giving nourishment is not a particularly difficult idea. It does not contradict the deeper ideas about sacrifice and death. These can fit into place when the questions are asked that need these answers.

At his Last Supper the Lord was not doing something completely new. He was transforming a familiar ordinary rite. The bread and the wine, blessed and divided between them, of which he said that evening "This is my body" and "This is my blood" already meant nourishment and companionship. A com-panion is a sharer of bread. So when he broke the bread and poured out the wine for the last time before he died, and told his followers to *do this* in his name, he was building on an existing foundation to give the bread and the wine an expanded meaning. They were to signify from now on his living and his dying for their sake.

The stories of Jesus feeding the people who crowded round to hear him when he taught are in all the Gospels[9] and have always been given a sacramental meaning. These narratives of a meal in the wilderness fit into the whole story by spelling out that Jesus took the bread as usual, that he "looked up to heaven, and blessed, and broke the loaves, and gave them

9. Matt 14:13–21; 15:32–38; Mark 6:35–44; Luke 9:12–17; John 6:5–14. Also Matt 15:32–38; Mark 8:1–9.

to the disciples to set before the people."[10] Must the accounts of the miraculous multiplication of the offered food be literal history, or could they be legendary development?[11] To insist on a definite answer can distract attention from the main point of these stories, which is the continuity between these portraits of Jesus in Galilee, when he ate and drank with his followers, and the developing life of the church, when they remembered his characteristic actions and obediently repeated them, inviting him to come among them. Christians confidently recollect their Lord as presiding over shared meals. They recognize his real presence when they break bread together in his name.

The supper in the upper room followed the familiar pattern, one more of many meals that Jesus and his disciples ate together: and indeed the Last Supper was not the last. St. Luke's Gospel tells that when he had died and risen he walked with two of them to Emmaus and "was known to them in the breaking of the bread."[12] At the end of the Fourth Gospel, it was when the risen Christ said "Come and have breakfast" that "they knew it was the Lord."[13]

The life, death, and rising of Jesus gave him the authority to give bread and wine their sacramental meaning, for his first disciples and for the generations following on. Austin Farrer said, "He gave them the sacrament by eating with them; he made it their salvation by his death."[14] Before he died, he ate real bread and drank real wine with his friends. He faced a death that was only too real. His rising on the third day established the faith of the church, that after all he was no defeated victim but the victorious Lord. Once again, the image of an arch, with its keystone put in place at last to stabilize what has been built already, is a good way of showing the structure of Christian belief, the faith of God's people validated by the Resurrection of Jesus Christ.[15]

Christians who celebrate the sacrament of the Eucharist, whether they think of themselves as Catholic or Protestant, can take hold of the idea of *real presence* to explain the meaning of what they are doing. They need not argue about the idea of "transubstantiation," the bread mysteriously turned into flesh while still looking like bread, whatever that means. The assurance

10. Mark 6:41.
11. See above, Chapter 6, 44.
12. Luke 24: 13–35.
13. John 21:9–14.
14. Farrer, *Eucharistic Theology Then and Now,* 31.
15. See above, Chapter 8, 59–60.

that the sacrament gives them is that the Lord himself will really come among them. Here is something that their hands can handle, which is a pledge that he will indeed be present with them.[16] When they look for continuity between the church today and the earthly life of the Son of God, here it is.

When Christians obediently celebrate the Eucharist, they are not morbidly re-enacting the horror that the Lord experienced once. Nor are they putting it out of their minds as long-ago history. What they are doing is using the symbols of broken bread and poured out wine to proclaim that his life was offered *for many*.[17] Whether or not they want to insist that he went through the suffering we deserve *instead* of us, the meaning is at least that he went through this suffering in order to be *with* us. God was in Christ,[18] taking part fully in the life and death of the human creatures God made.

Protestants reasonably suppose that the Giver of this precious gift wants people to receive it as a gift. They are not required to keep paying back what they owe by means of ritual sacrifices, especially as the whole point is that they cannot afford it. Rather than slaying the Lamb of God again and again as an offering on the altar, what Christians are meant to do is *give thanks* for his self-sacrifice, which is the meaning of Eucharist; and then go on to find out what they themselves can give, probably to other human beings. To offer oneself is to be ready to give what one can. Most people are not called to make the sacrifice of martyrdom, though some are, but every Christian is called to be what the Greek word "martyr" means, a witness to the faith.

For people who particularly value the sacrificial meaning of the Eucharist, there are words for them to use for entering into the offering of Christ. In *The Book of Common Prayer*, after receiving Communion, we offer "ourselves, our souls and bodies, to be a reasonable, holy, and lively sacrifice"; and *Common Worship* adds "through him." Christians believe that in their own lives they are invited to take part in the generosity of God the Son, in which he put himself without limit at the disposal of human beings. They are *recalling*, making present now, in a stronger sense than just remembering something that happened long ago, the one offering which he made, once for all, on the Cross.[19] They need not think that

16. 1 Cor 11:23–24.

17. Mark 14:24; Luke 22:20.

18. 2 Cor 5:19.

19. See Platten, "Reanimating Sacrifice?"

they are to kill him ritually again and again, as if they doubted his word that "It is finished."[20]

What Christians do re-enact, in order to belong to the Body of Christ, is his "table fellowship," which was not "once for all," but constantly renewed. If that is too much like pious jargon, its straightforward meaning is that they are allowed now to join in the eating and drinking together, the companionship of the Lord and his disciples. At the Eucharist they can gather up all the stories of the meals in Galilee, often with apparently unsuitable people.[21] Their Host is the risen Lord.

They may well be awestruck that in sharing this bread and this cup in this particular way they are coming into his presence and are themselves still continuing "in the apostles' doctrine and fellowship."[22] "The General Thanksgiving" in *The Book of Common Prayer* aptly identifies the heart of Christian gratitude. We bless God for "our creation, preservation and all the blessings of this life" indeed; but we give thanks "above all," not mainly for particular providences,[23] so much as for "the redemption of the world by our Lord Jesus Christ; for the means of grace, and for the hope of glory."

20. John 19:30 and also 17:4.

21. E.g., Luke 19:5–6.

22. Acts 2:42.

23. "The General Thanksgiving, in "Prayers and Thanksgivings, upon several Occasions", *The Book of Common Prayer.*

Part III

Behaving

15

Values, Human and Divine

> The new miracle of Christ's religion is the union
> of duty with delight.
>
> AUSTIN FARRER (1970), 137

MANY PEOPLE WHO COUNT themselves as Christians would not think of claiming that their lives are based upon anything as high-powered as the "doctrine and fellowship" of the apostles.[1] They are inclined to look on doctrine as academic and fellowship as cloying; and they would be embarrassed rather than gratified to be considered devout. They would prefer their Christianity to be identifiable by their moral convictions and their honest and kind-hearted behavior.

Even people who affirm the doctrine and are glad of the fellowship keep reverting to the stubborn notion that the main point of being a Christian is to distinguish what is right and practice it. How indeed could this not be so? Of course it must be values, moral values, which *matter most*: so it can look obvious that following Christ must mainly mean leading a Christian moral life. Then it is too easy to turn this round and assume that skeptics, who are not following Christ, must be morally adrift, with no real values. If goodness is so closely linked with faith, it is no wonder that Christians suppose that only believers have a firm foundation for their morality.

It needs to be reiterated that religious people have no monopoly of goodness. The distinctiveness of Christianity is not the morality that the

---

1. Acts 2:42.

Gospels preach but the facts that they teach. Believers assert, as a fact, that the universe has a Creator who is the Maker of all things. They offer as truth the statement that God brought the universe into being, setting in motion the slow natural processes that have produced human beings.

When they affirm, still as a matter of fact, that their God is not only supremely powerful but supremely good, they are speaking in terms that skeptics already understand. They expect people who do not believe in a Creator to take in what they are trying to say, even if they disagree. Just as someone does not have to believe in God already in order to comprehend and consider what Christians say about God's power, so believing is not a prior condition for recognizing what moral goodness means and understanding that in the Christian story God is good.

Whether anybody or anything is rightly identified as good depends upon what the facts are. Whether the universe is valuable as a whole depends upon what the whole truth about the universe turns out to be. The statement that there actually is a Creator of the universe might have been a morally neutral assertion, that it just so happened, whether we like it or not, that the Big Bang was detonated like a firework by a powerful Deity. Believers have more to say about what the Creator is like. Some human beings testify to their experiences of encountering a personal Reality they call God, who shows the superlative goodness which they can recognize as *holy*.

The good news affirmed by Christians is that indeed it is love that "makes the world go round'": as Dante put it, the love "which moves the sun and the other stars."[2] God created the universe for the sake of the creatures who would live in it. These wanted creatures were made to be loved and to love. Christians go on to declare that God has not only brought human beings into existence. God has undertaken the harder responsibility of saving them.[3] People who believe that these witnesses are trustworthy find themselves called to throw in their lot with them. They go beyond merely believing *that* there is a God to believing *in* God, putting their faith in God.[4]

If Christians commending their faith are so possessive about the notion of goodness that they do not even expect people who lack faith to understand what they are saying, they can hardly expect to be believed. Human beings have evolved, long before there was a gospel, to recognize important values, to mind about them, and to be able to share them.

2. Dante, *Paradiso,* Canto 13, line 96.
3. See "God's responsibility" under "God" in the Index.
4. See above, Chapter 8, 57.

Christians therefore need not belittle the moral notions of their contemporaries. Believers and skeptics can look together at the factual and ethical questions, inquiring what is true about the universe, what matters and what to do about it.

The right ways of life for human flourishing are based upon what people and the physical world are like, not on what anyone, even God, has decided to command.[5] What the Creator decided, believers assert, was to make and cherish creatures like these and bring them to fulfilment. God said first, "Let there be light"; and then, "Let us make man in our image";[6] not, "Let there be ethics." "And God saw everything that he had made, and behold, it was very good."[7]

If the story of the one forbidden fruit stood on its own as a divine taboo, it would be harder for believers to find common ethical cause with unbelievers. The story which goes on to tell of the Ten Commandments and the Torah reveals comprehensible moral duties as the needful requirements for sustaining human well-being. The deep-rooted idea of "natural law" makes sense, whether there is a divine Lawgiver or whether there is not. H. L. A. Hart, who was Professor of Jurisprudence in the University of Oxford, pointed out[8] that laws have developed in their particular forms in order to protect our human life together. For a set of rules to be recognizable as a moral code, it cannot consist of arbitrary or haphazard regulations. Morality necessarily includes "some form of prohibition of the use of violence, to persons or things, and requirements of truthfulness, fair dealing, and respect for promises." So he found here "a core of indisputable truth in the doctrines of Natural Law."[9]

A conspicuous example of how the facts of what human beings are like has given rise to rule-governed arrangements for people's well-being is the characteristic human institution of marriage. Human beings are pairbonding animals.[10] Men and women are capable of binding themselves in faithful lifelong bonds, and of finding happiness in so doing; and this capacity does not depend upon whether or not they believe in God. Some of us have long resisted the possessiveness which claims "*Christian* marriage" as the

---

5. See above, Chapter 3, 22.

6. Gen 1:3 and 1:26.

7. Gen 1:31.

8. Hart, *The Concept of Law*, 176.

9. Ibid.

10. See Oppenheimer, *Marriage*, especially Chapter 2.

only authentic union of a man and a woman, as if the marriage bond were church property and matrimony without the gospel counted for nothing.

Christian moralists might learn likewise to resist the more comprehensive possessiveness that claims "*Christian* ethics" as the only valid way to think about goodness, as if they could consign all the inhabitants of ancient societies, along with modern unbelievers, to a moral desert empty of values. I like to call the faith I hold Christian humanism,[11] because I am glad to share with skeptical humanists the awareness that real moral values are based upon the needful conditions for human flourishing. Ethics would still apply to human living were there no divine Authority to promulgate moral decrees and enforce them with rewards and punishments. I am certain at least that my human life is shared with other people and that my flourishing is bound up with theirs. We differ about whether there is a God who made us, who cares about our happiness and who shows us how to find it; but we can go a long way together.

Yet the first Christians did call their faith *the way*. Followers of Christ had a distinctive route to follow. They were not to fit in comfortably with skeptics and be conformed to the world.[12] Does loyalty require faithful Christians now to abandon the ways of their fellow travelers and set off in an entirely different direction? They may well think that some of the companions they would like to have with them on their journey are going the wrong way and need a more reliable map. They might apply the metaphor more generously, not by abandoning the others and leaving them behind, but by making the effort to share the available resources, with a lively hope of arriving together at the same destination, a place they will all eventually recognize, not an alien territory.

If faith refrains from claiming ownership of morality, "being good" can make the same kind of sense for believers and unbelievers. A Christian humanist can stand on the same ground as skeptical humanists. It does not follow that provided morality is secure, piety can be reckoned as no more than an optional extra, which some people may like to take up as a sort of hobby. What religious faith adds to the ethics we can all share is belief that in fact there really is a good and holy Power, who affirms and sustains our best aspirations; who will ultimately vindicate the moral values that belong to the well-being of the creatures we are.

11. See above, Chapter 3, 23.

12. Rom 12:2.

Errant human beings can and do aspire to be good, but their aspirations are not likely to be successful unaided. Christians have the assurance that the moral life does not have to be "all one's own work." God's people have been taught all along what values matter most and how to set about putting them into practice, so as to become good human beings. The lessons are summarized in the Ten Commandments and transformed in the Sermon on the Mount. The pupils are not left to find the way on their own, but are given experiences of grace to which they can respond. The Psalmist did not find God's law a burden. It was "more to be desired than gold: . . . sweeter also than honey and the honeycomb."[13]

Though faith does not plant values in the world, it nourishes them. The goodness that Christians preach and try to practice develops by being well watered and brought to fruition. The image of reaping a harvest was important to St. Paul. "Love, joy, peace, patience, kindness, goodness, faithfulness, gentleness, self-control" are not a consignment of goods addressed and delivered to the church, but the maturing "fruit of the Spirit."[14] St. Paul would surely have repudiated any notion that the church can put a fence around the territory of the Spirit and claim every plant that grows.[15]

The distinctiveness that does belong to the morality of Christians is not a matter of growing a different crop in a field of their own, but of preparing for a remarkable harvest. Because Christians believe that God's goodness is infinite, the goodness that God intends for humanity is unlimited. Followers of Christ are expected to go beyond, to *transcend*, the standard requirements of human ethics. The moral demands of faith are unbounded. If God is not only good but holy, God's beloved creatures are offered the prospect that they are to be not only good but holy.[16]

How can it be somebody's duty to go beyond duty? Since fairness is not enough, and Christians are commanded to transcend the good behavior that can justly be required of them, must they admit that God's demands are unreasonably difficult? The paradoxical answer is that transcendent morality is not difficult: it is either impossible or easy. People can become able to set aside the apparatus of rights and duties and to go beyond ordinary reasonable moral expectation, when they are given glimpses of glory. The distinctive shape of Christian ethics is a pattern of offer and response.

13. Ps 19:10.

14. Gal 5:22–23.

15. E.g., Rom 2:14–15.

16. Matt 5:48; Heb 12:23.

First God shows people something and then, in response, they come to see what they must do. When people say that it is high time we went back to the Ten Commandments, they should consider how the Ten Commandments arrived. "I am the Lord your God, who brought you out of the land of Egypt."[17] God's actions came before God's demands.

Vocations start with visions. The God whom Jews and Christians worship "remembered his covenant with Abraham, with Isaac, and with Jacob,"[18] and appeared to Moses "in a flame of fire out of the midst of a bush,"[19] to send this shy man to rescue the people from their oppressors. The prophet Isaiah was in the Temple at a time of unhappy discouragement, the year that the good King Uzziah died. [20] He received a vision of the Lord, high and lifted up, surrounded by seraphim crying "Holy, holy, holy." Aware of being unworthy, "a man of unclean lips," he was forthwith commissioned to take God's message to God's people; and that message has been passed on through twenty-eight centuries. When the time came for the Christian gospel to be preached, the pattern of divine action and human response decisively took shape, when God came in person to live a human life and die and rise. It was the risen Christ, when he came back to the disheartened disciples, who had the authority to send them out as apostles.

There should still be no Christian takeover bid. The pattern of being "taken out of oneself" is still recognizably characteristic of human beings, not reserved for believers. Christians have no monopoly in generosity, nor even in grace. People are often responsive, kind, magnanimous, devoted. To love somebody else "as oneself" need not be heroic nor even extraordinary. Human kindness, even though patchy, limited, and selective, is real and valid; and believers in God can find here a small-scale model of divine love. When people are growing a harvest of goodwill they are able, even in quite normal circumstances, to go beyond "Do I have to?" and cheerfully exceed expectations.[21] Commonsense tells them not to keep pulling the crop up by the roots to check how it is growing, but to get on hopefully with the work in hand. Time is on their side when they are letting fulfilment steal up on them at its own pace, rather than fretting over achieving set goals.

17. Exod 20:2.
18. Exod 2:24.
19. Exod 3:2–6, 11–12.
20. Isa 6:1–8.
21. See Farrer, chapter heading above.

The gospel does not mainly consist of instructions about how people are to behave when all is going well, but of hope provided for when they fail. The particular message of Christianity is that when human love is at a loss, when people really do not want to be kind, magnanimous, or loving, God's love, the sort of love Christ taught and showed in his life and death and validated in his rising, is still "on offer" inviting response, not legalistic but welcoming.

16

The Way

"After all," said the duchess vaguely, "there are certain things you can't get away from. Right and wrong, good conduct and moral rectitude, have certain well-defined limits."

"So, for the matter of that," replied Reginald, "has the Russian Empire. The trouble is that the limits are not always in the same place."

SAKI, "REGINALD AT THE THEATRE"

PEOPLE WHO BELIEVE THAT God's goodness claims human response are bound to do something about it. Response is not indefinite approval but identifiable positive behavior. Christians who have faith in Jesus of Nazareth as the Son of God have the New Testament accounts of the Lord's life and teaching to show them the way to live as children of the heavenly Father. They are still to avoid jumping to the conclusion that Jesus taught his disciples the meaning of "right" and "wrong." Nor had Moses in his day given the chosen people their first moral notions, when he summed up God's will for them in Ten Commandments. Human beings recognize values without a special messenger from God to inaugurate their ethics; and real duties can stand up apart from divine backing.[1]

1. See above, Chapter 3, 22 and Chapter 15, 115.

When the Lord Jesus came, he declared the scale and scope of goodness in God's sight and inspired people to come in. He taught by using stories and images, opening up the meaning of heavenly goodness and bringing the truth about God's generosity newly into focus for anyone who would listen.[2] All sorts of people came crowding round this new prophet to hear what he would say, before there was a Christian church identifying its own members by drawing moral boundaries around the ones who belonged, at the risk of leaving the others out in the cold.

His two outstanding images are the kingdom of God, and the heavenly Father. The beginning of the good news of Jesus Christ[3] was that God's kingdom was at hand, a government with a different spirit from the warlike Roman rule only too familiar to his hearers. Even more characteristically, he identified God the King with God the Father. The two images complement one another, the awesomeness of the exalted ruler balanced by the ordinary familiarity of the affectionate parent. Each image invites particular attention to God's special concern for the small people who are not to be disregarded and need to be cherished.

The distinctive authority of Jesus the teacher comes from the history of his living, dying, and rising. His followers are bound to tell the whole story,[4] not reducing the Lord to a moralist whose main intent was to uphold the best ethical standards. The reason for his coming was not to legislate for God's people. Nobody whose top priority was establishing rules for virtuous behaviour would have chosen to tell the stories he told or to keep the company he kept. He did not play safe morally, but took what any right-minded person could see were great risks. He enlivened his teaching with paradox, exaggeration, and humor, even with teasing.[5] When people imagine Jesus Christ as characteristically solemn and judgmental, they miss the light-hearted happiness of the good news.

We have no tape recording of his speech. Context and tone of voice, now lost for ever, make a huge difference to meaning. Christians have never found it easy to reckon with stories such as the laborers who worked all day and received no more pay in the end than the ones who started late,[6] or the unjust steward who solved his problem by cheating his master and was

2. E.g., Matt 13:9; Mark 4:9; Luke 8:8.

3. Mark 1:1 and 14–15.

4. See above, Chapter 9, 67.

5. E.g., Matt 16:25; 18:8–9; 19:24; Luke 18:25; Mark 3:17.

6. Matt 20:1–16.

not condemned but commended for it.[7] Among all the notions that people think are "Christian ethics," one thing is clear: Jesus was far from encouraging legalism. It does not look at all as if the teacher's message was about maintaining strict standards of morality. Time-honored human tradition might even turn out to make the void the word of God.[8]

The Christian answer to ethical questioning is less likely to be a plain stern prohibition, "Thou shalt not," than a bold positive directive, "Go the whole way." Moralists who reduce ethics to conscientiousness cut lively morality down to lifeless priggish moralism. People assert too easily, "What we need is standards." Often it is not practicing Christians who say it, but people on the edge of the church who care about the parlous state of the world, who are upset at the thought that Christians in authority are letting everyone down by not giving us the moral lead we lack. But the Gospel accounts of the Lord's teaching may well seem to undermine standards rather than upholding them.

The keeping of the Sabbath was an important standard. The Pharisees were the ones who were faithfully maintaining it. Two thousand years later, Christians are used to the idea that the Pharisees had their priorities all wrong, but now with that lesson thoroughly learnt, it is fair to remember that the Pharisees indeed had a point: the same point as the serious people who say today, for instance, that there can be no remarriage after divorce. "This will create a wrong impression and betray our values."

Which are the ones who are on the Lord's side now? The argument moves to and fro between over-simplifications. Kind-hearted people who set store by tolerance find the liberal message congenial, that real disciples are unconventional and permissive, doing away with harsh rules and regulations. Their gentle Jesus, who meekly and mildly says "Never mind" to sinners, is as imaginary as the legislating Jesus. Broad-mindedness is not the whole gospel and has to keep making room for the sterner emphasis, that true Christians are loyally conservative. That is the message that is congenial to people who realize how dependent their historic faith is upon their heroic predecessors. Disciples are naturally somewhat traditional, because if they give way to permissiveness they cut off the branch on which they need to sit.

But then, when followers of Christ take the stricter message so readily to heart, they revert to being latter day Pharisees. In the name of loyal

7. Luke 16:1–8.
8. Matt 15:6.

integrity, they harden their minds and shun woolly liberalism, thinking of themselves as steadfast when really they are being legalistic. Unless they beware of the tempting comfort of keeping everything tidy with precise regulations, their faithfulness slides into bigotry. If conscientious disciples on both sides could dare to be less confident that their understanding is the whole truth, they might build more reliably together on what they have understood so far.

They may try out the appealing idea that there are two standards of morality, a basic lower level for all and an advanced level for some. The world is content to do this, but we do that. So kindly Christians have permission to be gentle with other people's shortcomings, but each one has to keep saying firmly, "As for me and my house, we will serve the Lord."[9] But efforts to apply this promising distinction show that the policy of being always hard on oneself and soft with other people is really no more Christian than unbending strictness, though it is more subtly misleading. If I imagined the Lord making exalted demands upon *me* but not really minding what *you* do, the gospel would hardly be good news for either of us.

Dutiful Christians who care about tradition will find, if they attend to the New Testament, how radical this tradition of theirs is. The church began among people who were hoping for a Messiah, a Christ. The Messiah came; but the manner of his coming and what happened, and the way he refounded the tradition that his followers maintain through the centuries, were all quite unexpected. It would be strange to suppose that God has nothing new in store for his people any more. It is more reverent to trust in a God who may surprise us than to suppose that we have the Almighty taped.

A good deal of Christian loyalty to unchanging tradition looks like an attempt to protect God from being let down by liberals. Some of the anxiety people are feeling about loss of standards is based on a notion that God will be shocked if people allow their moral beliefs to develop and change, as if our Heavenly Father were an Aged Parent who will be upset unless each generation keeps everything going on in the same good old way. But the Christian gospel is not about things going on in the same old way. God is less timid than human moralists and more inclined to take risks. The Son of God when he came took great risks of being misunderstood, both in his teaching and in his behavior. What happened was the Cross, when it all went horribly wrong, and the Resurrection, when God gloriously brought good out of evil. That is the characteristic pattern of Christian belief.

9. Josh 24:15.

So likewise the shape of Christian ethics turns out to be more risky than careful conformity to settled moral principles. Christians do God's will by entering into the divine pattern of generous offer and grateful response.[10] The key word is "therefore." "God is like this: therefore we are to be like this." That was the basis of St. Paul's teaching to the young churches. Our Lord Jesus Christ "died for us so that . . . we might live with him. *Therefore* encourage one another and build one another up, just as you are doing":[11] indeed, one may notice, just as St. Paul himself was doing.

Tolerant moralists, who dare to sit lightly to fixed standards, do run the risk of preaching "cheap grace"; but it is more dangerous to preach grudging grace. People quickly pick up the message that God is mean. If they have broken the rules, or even if they have not seen the point of the rules, they are not wanted and God's church is not for them. That is a travesty of Christian belief, but a travesty that persists. Some loyal Christians never see the harm they do by their unimaginative confidence. The people they fail to welcome do not stay and argue: they simply go away, and stop expecting the church of Christ to have any blessings to offer to them or their families. Secure well-behaved Christians ought to ask why the sinners welcomed Jesus to their festivities, why there were apt to be children around him, why there was no need to make sure there was a good turnout when he preached, and why the most pious people were the ones who found his message objectionable.

Traditionalists challenge permissive liberals: surely morality demands strict adherence to unchangeable standards? What is right in the sight of God cannot shift with human opinions but must be permanently established. The liberal defense against this charge of dangerous woolly-mindedness is to point out that what does keep changing is not the moral law, but the states of affairs in which moral laws are put into effect. When the facts have changed, the application of a given ethical standard yields different practical guidance. Morality always demands fairness, responsibility, loyalty, generosity . . . ; but new terms of reference produce new problems and new answers about what people ought therefore to do.

Christians do not always find it easy to believe the hymn many of them sang in their youth, that "new occasions" really may "teach new duties."[12] St.

10. See above, Chapter 15, 117–18.

11. 1 Thess 5:10–11.

12. James Russell Lowell, "Once to Every Man and Nation Comes the Moment to Decide," in *The Present Crisis.*

Peter, instructed in a vision to prepare and eat unclean meat, protested in alarm: "not so, Lord."[13] How could the ancient God-given food laws, which he had loyally kept, ever become obsolete? He was able to take his place in history as the first Christian bishop, not in spite of his yielding, but on the contrary because he did grasp the new situation and applied the lesson, bravely taking the radical step of welcoming Cornelius the Roman centurion into the Christian church.

Jewish Christians still went on asking whether these acceptable Gentile converts must be circumcised, in order to enter into membership of God's people. The answer the church reached was hard-won. It was a potentially destructive controversy that the Council of Jerusalem[14] had to face, and which they solved in principle, allowing the welcoming solution to be worked out in practice.

St. Paul wrote[15] that in Christ "there is no longer Jew or Greek, there is no longer slave or free, there is no longer male or female"; and concentrated in particular on the first of these insights. "Jew or Greek" was the split whose healing he was called to take in hand. "No longer slave or free" aroused the Christian conscience many centuries later; and it is only now that "no longer male or female" is coming into its own, not without strenuous controversy. Among the most pressing problems and difficulties in our day are intractable problems concerning sexual ethics, which are presenting themselves insistently and seem unlikely to go away.

A parish group was invited, as a light-hearted Lenten exercise, to suggest commandments that should be broken. One could think of compulsive rules, made for the sake of piety, which one can permit oneself cheerfully to leave behind for the sake of maturity. "Always fast before receiving Communion." More fundamentally, the question could lead followers of the Christian way today to look around them and ask whether the morality they are doggedly practicing and calling "Christian" is attracting or repelling the next generation of God's children. Is it time to be less confident that the church is rightly interpreting God's unchanging will?

In the twentieth century many states of affairs changed, inviting fresh moral insights. For example, people nowadays can make love to one another without expecting to conceive a child. The lifting of that ancient relentless pressure has made a convincing difference to what ways of living can be

13. Acts 10:11–15.
14. Acts 15.
15. Gal 3:28.

allowed, and even recommended, as responsible, fair, loyal, and loving. We need not discount the specific moral judgments of our ancestors as wrong then, for we realize that our situation is different.

The commandment, "Be fruitful and multiply" has been well obeyed. The earth is only too thoroughly replenished with human beings. Heaven forbid that God's people should become ungrateful for the excellent blessing of a large family; but if everyone keeps claiming that blessing in an over-populated world, the damage will be catastrophic. To realize that contraception is also a blessing is no sin, but has become an urgent imperative. People who now can and should put less emphasis on procreation as the primary purpose of the human pairbond value as much as ever the mutual help, society, and comfort that spouses can give to one another; and they may find themselves in a better position to develop these encouragements.

Because young people's passions are no longer as hazardous as they once were, older people who have prudently conformed to stricter rules should be glad now to take up, and gracefully apply to the moral behavior of the present younger generation, Wordsworth's insight in his "Ode to Duty":

> There are who ask not if thine eye
> Be on them; who in love and truth,
> Where no misgiving is, rely
> Upon the genial sense of youth; . . .
> Oh! If through confidence misplaced
> They fail, thy saving arms, dread Power! around them cast.

Christians are now at risk, in newfound tolerance, of redirecting their intolerance, not blaming their adventurous juniors but hastily blaming their predecessors whose moral assumptions now look harsh. It is as necessary as ever to use one's imagination, to understand what mattered so much in the old days. To take heed now of more variegated points of view is both responsibility and opportunity.

Sometimes it remains clear that flexibility can be overdone and that to break an old commandment is a plain temptation to be resisted. The seven deadly sins are still truly perilous, though they are neither unforgivable nor the whole story about moral duty. But when disciples of Christ are actually not at all tempted to commit adultery or perjury, they have to face the different temptation of becoming trapped in righteous conformity to their valued rules. A besetting sin of devout people, rather than defiant disobedience, is obsessiveness, small-minded obstinacy disguising itself as faithfulness.

Instead of God's law being found sweeter than honey,[16] the making and enforcing of regulations can become a sour idolatry. Christians are required to keep looking critically at their current stubborn ethical certainties, which are dividing the church and positively antagonizing the world.

More controversially than the value of birth control, Christians might begin to look more favorably upon dedicated same-sex partnerships as at least akin to marriages. Would it now be generous, not disloyal but even overdue, to recognize these unions as valid and valuable, though they lack the fruitfulness of procreation? Traditionalists point out truthfully that what "marriage" means is the joining of a man and a woman, and rest content in their honest use of language; but making a stand here, as if applying this definition were the whole answer, begins to look more and more like making void the word of God by our tradition.[17]

To ask whether Christians are really commanded to go on refusing God's grace to same-sex fidelity is not a rhetorical question, but has become an urgent inquiry about what ways of life God might bless, in a world which cannot sustain more and more people. Just as happily married Christians, who have no axe of their own to grind, have been opening their minds to other people's matrimonial troubles, and working to improve the law of divorce, so contentedly heterosexual Christians are starting to consider cautiously whether the ancient teachings of the church about gender and sexual love are still conveying the whole truth about God's purposes.

It would be confusing, and even unethical, to change the definition of "marriage," but charity commands Christians to find and adopt a satisfactory vocabulary, less drearily bureaucratic than "civil partnership," for sincere lifestyles they must stop calling perverted. People who would gladly combine honorable principle with benign goodwill could recognize same-sex unions as truly a kind of *covenant*, fit to be affirmed as such with blessings and celebration. The problem is not trivial. Unless Christians at least make an effort to find and use a friendly workable terminology, the world will have some reason for regarding church people as so many quarrelling children.

> Let dogs delight to bark and bite
> For God has made them so . . .
> Your little hands were never made
> To tear out each other's eyes.[18]

16. Ps 19:10. See above, Chapter 15, 117.

17. See 122n8.

18. Isaac Watts, "Against Quarrelling."

The ethics of sex have never been the heart of Christian ethics, certainly not according to the gospel accounts of the teaching of Christ. It is high time that Christians made more effort to correct that false impression. Then sexual morality could take its valued place as one conspicuous area where Christian understanding can indeed shed light on the Christian way, showing part of the meaning of love. The Christian church is better placed today to receive this illumination, leaving behind persistent ingrained sexism, and also learning to outgrow the ancient moral hostility to the body that now looks like a plain aberration. Appreciation of the whole embodied person, for which the word "holism" has become a fashionable keyword, once used to be a luxury for fortunate civilized individuals in comfortable circumstances. In a world with more advanced medical expertise, better hygiene and modern plumbing, it has become realistic to stop expecting the body to be an enemy of the soul, and to allow matter and spirit to be more happily related in human lives.

17

Compare and Contrast

> . . . the mighty God, the everlasting Father,
> the Prince of Peace.
>
> ISAIAH 9:6

TWENTY-FIRST CENTURY CHRISTIANS ARE trying to follow the way of Christ, who lived on earth two thousand years ago. If we know anything about Jesus of Nazareth beyond the facts that he was crucified and is proclaimed as the Lord who rose from death, we know that he was a teacher, and that his most characteristic method of teaching was by using stories and images.[1] Far from blurring the distinction between truth and falsity, he could tell the truth in this way more vividly and memorably.[2] Figures of speech can be as true or as false as prose, and similes do not have to compete with one another to be the correct one. Diverse images stand side by side in the scriptures, each shedding its own light on what Christians believe about God.[3]

The two images at the heart of the good news that Christ preached are the *kingdom of God*, and the *heavenly Father*. When Christians obediently pray, "Thy kingdom come," their prayer has begun, as Jesus taught them,[4] by addressing God as "Our Father." Their Creed that proclaims their faith

1. See above, Chapter 16, 121.
2. See above, Chapter 6, 43.
3. See above, Chapter 9, 64.
4. Matt 6:9f; Luke 11:2.

accordingly starts with this boldly naive image: "I believe in one God the Father Almighty."

There is no doubt that if there is indeed a God, then God is the King of the universe. The teaching of Christ began with God's rule: "The time is fulfilled, and the kingdom of God is at hand."[5] "God the Father" is the more distinctive image, which Christians claim as their very own.[6] Richard Bauckham points out that "Outside the parables, Jesus never calls God 'King' and very rarely 'Lord.'"[7] In using the image of Father, he says, "Jesus was taking up a thoroughly Jewish way of thinking of God but privileging it over others."[8]

Before Christ came and taught, the Hebrew scriptures already set the images of kingly authority and parental care alongside one another. The Lord's mercy to those who fear him is like the mercy of a father to his children.[9] The God who "rideth upon the heavens, as it were upon a horse" is "a Father of the fatherless, and defendeth the cause of the widows."[10] When the Psalmist says, "and forget not all his benefits,"[11] he is not reminding himself of the Social Security payments he is entitled to claim: he is pondering the compassion of a father who "pities his own children."[12]

There is no need to ask whether God is King or Father, any more than one need ask whether a human ruler is a king or a father. The author of this book, more at home in family life than in the world of government, is inclined to give most emphasis to the analogy of God's parenthood. It would need another book, written by somebody with political understanding sustained by New Testament scholarship, to redress this one-sidedness and give due weight to the biblical image of God's kingdom, keeping these two given metaphors properly in balance.

Reverent piety feels comfortable with the image of God the King, which emphasizes the awesome *contrast* between the Almighty Creator and human rulers. Reverent gratitude is able to grasp and keep holding on to the permitted *comparison* between God the Father's grace and human

---

5. Mark 1:15.

6. See Oppenheimer, *On Being Someone*, Chapter 16.

7. Bauckham, *Jesus, A Very Short Introduction*, 64.

8. Ibid., 65

9. Ps 103:13.

10. Ps 68: 4–5.

11. Ps 103:2.

12. Ps 103: 8, 13.

love, especially the ordinary recognizable kind of love that human creatures show to their own offspring.

Calling God "Father" affirms that the way children matter to their parents is a fit image of the way human beings matter to the Creator who brought the universe into being. The children of the heavenly Father are sure that they have his full attention and can ask him confidently for what they need.[13] Christians may well find it remarkable that they are allowed to address their holy God in such a familiar way. They ought to take this image of parental love thoroughly to heart, in order to scotch the legalistic notions that religious people too readily develop about how God deals with humanity.

Whatever behavior parents expect of good children, avoiding adult wrath and earning favors are not the best ways to describe what is going on. Human affection, given and reciprocated, must be a better analogy than bargains negotiated, for showing the meaning of God's grace and human response. The weariness, the impatience, and the ordinary selfishness that beset human family life have to be subtracted, but the cherishing, the brave hopes and the enthusiasm are to be recognized as divine. Parents can understand, more easily than clergy or theologians, that their role is not to make their children conform to some standard, but to develop each child's best self.

The Lord's disciples can put his teaching about becoming like children into practice by asking as straightforwardly as children do for what they really want. They may need reminding to say "Please" and "Thank you" like good children. It is piously trite, but realistic, to say that sometimes the answer has to be "No" or "Wait"; and often it turns out to be "Hush and listen." Young children can hardly have reliable notions of what they really need. They soon grow old enough to be encouraged to put into words what they would like, and hope sometimes to be given it just because they have asked. There is an interplay between parental responsibility and the children's own ideas and hopes. They take part in their own upbringing.

Christians apply the teaching about becoming as little children by daring to speak naively about God's Fatherhood. Instead of patronizing the Psalmist who bluntly upbraided the Almighty, "Up, Lord, why sleepest thou,"[14] they can picture the God of their tradition as a human parent, who sometimes withdraws, and themselves as children approaching their father and clamoring for him to attend to them. Prayer is not supposed to be im-

13. E.g., Matt 6:6, 26, 32; 7:11; Luke 11:11–13; 12:29–32.

14. Ps 44:23.

personal, still less mechanical. Children whose wishes were granted with cool anonymous regularity would be orphans missing the special blessing of individual care.

Christians indeed have a story about gaining the Lord's attention. When they tell one another that Jesus commanded the obedience of the wind and the waves, instead of teaching one simple lesson about faith in God's power they might pick up a particular detail, "But he was in the stern, asleep on the cushion."[15] His frightened disciples have to wake him up, and then they are awestruck at his response.[16]

Christian disciples today are well aware that their heavenly Father may withdraw. If none of them ever had any particular experience of God's grace near at hand, sustaining and inspiring them, Christian faith might well wither. The claim to recognize, sometimes, glimpses of God's fatherly presence is not an optional extra. A responsible Christian is bound to look for some positive awareness of heavenly grace, sometimes arriving by sudden revelation, more often by people sharing their experience of small accumulating hints and hopes, gradually identifiable.[17] As they explore the world, would-be believers are not always left to find their own way. They can be members of a body of people, showing one another reasons for trusting that the heavenly Father is on their side, even when they have hard lessons to learn.

When human parenthood is pondered as the best image of God, realistic limits can be set to the persistent notion that believers ought to have faith in divine providence controlling the whole course of history, so that nothing can ever really go wrong. Parents have to realize that they cannot, and should not, look after their children by taking charge of every detail of their experience. They may therefore be ready to understand that God's grace cannot be expected to arrange everything in ways that human beings want. The processes of the natural world must be dependably stable and continue of their own accord in their generally predictable but not always manageable ways, or they would not provide the necessary context in which people can grow and develop.[18]

Yet the image of God as the heavenly Father may cautiously allow for enough play in the system, enough flexibility in the steady sequence

15. Mark 4:38.

16. Mark 4:41.

17. See above, Chapter 13, 96, and note 5 there; and 99.

18. See above, Chapter 11, 82–3.

of events, for some happenings, not all and probably not even many, to be given as God's special blessing or as God's particular calling. It is unnecessary to suppose that the natural universe is made up entirely of lifeless machinery, or that a Christian may never dare to be grateful for God's singular kindness for fear of rash wishful thinking.

Believers are understandably afraid of taking God's loving care for granted and presuming upon the image of the heavenly Father, of being over-familiar with "the high and lofty one who inhabits eternity, whose name is Holy."[19] This is a risk that Jesus evidently allowed and indeed encouraged his disciples to take. When they ask like children for what they want[20] the answer may not be "Yes" but it will not be, "Don't be impertinent." "Our courteous Lord," said Julian of Norwich, "wants us to be as friendly with him as the heart may conceive or the soul may desire. But be careful," she added, "not to take this friendliness too casually, so that we neglect courtesy; for our Lord himself is supreme friendliness, and he is as courteous as he is friendly; for he is truly courteous."[21]

As a corrective to presuming upon the dignity of being a member of God's family, the equally biblical image of adoption comes into view. The royal status of a child of God is neither inborn nor earned, but granted. People are made God's children by adoption and grace, "and if children, then heirs, heirs of God and fellow heirs with Christ."[22] The people so honored may well turn out to be the unacceptable people whom others reject.

For believers, this teaching is thoroughly encouraging, but hostile critics are ready to attack. It is all very well to make these confident assertions that we have a loving Father in heaven who is on our side. Many human beings, sadly or bitterly, feel forced to deny this.[23] God is evidently not to be found in the midst of the family, like an earthly father who has come home in time to play with the children. They are supposed to trust their heavenly Father, but they cannot "climb his knee the envious kiss to share."[24] Faith in God can be unsympathetically presented as a series of speculative assumptions, first asserting God's reality, on no adequate grounds; and then going on to insist, however improbable it may seem, that the invisible silent God is best

---

19. Isa 57:15.

20. See note 13 above.

21. Julian of Norwich, *Revelations of Divine Love*, Chapter 77.

22. Rom 8:14–17; Gal 4:4–7

23. See above, Chapter 4, 28.

24. Gray, "Elegy Written in a Country Churchyard," Line 24, *Poems*.

described as "Father." Christian belief can seem too much like climbing a flight of wobbly steps in the dark.

Faith would hardly be persuasive if it simply announced, "There is a God who made us," propounding this assertion as a bare statement, perhaps with some academic interest in its own right; adding on only later, as a further step, a description of what we hope the Creator is like, which then turns out to have moral implications for everyone. The doctrine of creation could not stand up as an intellectual exercise apart from people's everyday concerns, as one might study the heavens and find out that Jupiter has at least thirteen moons. Belief that everything depends upon God is a whole worldview, offered as the most convincing way of interpreting value-laden human experience. Theology cannot be ethically neutral, but includes all along some significant information about the moral character of this God in whom we are invited to have faith.

The story of creation starts, "In the beginning God created the heavens and the earth."[25] It is a direct development of the same story, that the Maker of the universe is holy and good, and commands human beings to do justly and love mercy and walk humbly with their God.[26] Christian faith takes up the narrative and leads on to the dénouement that our Creator is the God and Father of our Lord Jesus Christ, who takes responsibility for earthly creatures, to the extent of forgiving their sins and bearing the cost of their wrongdoings. Believers have not self-indulgently developed this story because it encourages them to feel hopeful. The evidence they offer that God is holy, and has been revealed as generous, is not their own invention but has been provided by particular historical happenings. Christians find the good news trustworthy, that Jesus of Nazareth was the Son of God, who was born at a particular time, lived a human life, taught about God as the Father, died, and rose again; and they pass this narrative on to one another.

Christian statements of fact and Christian ethics are connected parts of one account of the world: that the universe was created by God; that God loves human beings as a father loves his children; and that Christian behavior is the way people live who belong to God's family. To keep attending to the teaching that the Lord gave to his first disciples, taking hold of his image of the heavenly Father, can help to counteract some of the cruel or legalistic notions about how God deals with humanity that seem to beset some Christians as much as anyone.

25. Gen 1:1.
26. Mic 6:8.

To use the image with confidence, some clarification is needed. First, it would be tempting nowadays to be sidetracked on to the Father versus Mother argument. If some people want to address our God as Mother, following indeed the example of Julian,[27] they evidently have insights to offer, though many of us would choose not to abandon the traditional language. It would surely be worthwhile to make more use of the maternal imagery that the scriptures do provide;[28] but that is not the present point. What matters first is to take to heart the idea that the God of our tradition is on our side, as parents are on their children's side.

Secondly, to call God Father does not have much to do with something called "Christian family life" with its plain assumptions about what Christian living should be like, which is liable to leave people who are not provided with that sort of family out in the cold. There is not a great deal of teaching about family life in the Gospels, and some of it is quite negative.[29] Calling God Father is not a matter of specifying domestic arrangements, but of approaching the Almighty as children approach their parents. This needs to be made clear, because Christians are too apt to present their Deity more forbiddingly.

Thirdly, the purpose of using this authoritative image is not to preach a sermon about imitating the trustfulness of little children. Christians offering the image of the heavenly Father are not telling one another how to behave, but explaining part of the meaning of their doctrine of God. When believers make theological statements that ignore God's Fatherhood, their doctrine is not so much wrong as lopsided. Like the Pharisees, they say true things that mislead. The awareness that God our Creator is holy leads easily to the notion that the Almighty will always be a stern judge when anyone goes astray. The conviction that God is indeed the Almighty leads easily to the notion that everything that happens, however unwelcome, must be what he wants, as if people ought to be thankful even for what makes them miserable. The belief that God has given us laws for our good leads easily to the notion that we ought to worship an impersonal heavenly bureaucrat, who is more concerned about our keeping the rules than about our happiness. So some of the most loyal Christians present their God as judgmental, tyrannical, legalistic.

---

27. Julian of Norwich, *Revelations of Divine Love*, Chapter 77.
28. E.g., Matt 23:37; Luke 13:34; 1 Cor 3:1–2
29. E.g., Matt 12:48; Mark 3:33; Luke 8:20.

To redress the balance, less alarming attributes of God need emphasis. The message Jesus came into Galilee preaching was not "Repent and tremble," but "Repent and believe in the good news."[30] What sense would the Gospels make without the idea of the Father who cares about the family?[31] The holy God is not sitting grandly on high, testing people and blaming them. We should not imagine the heavenly Father as always angry, but even as sometimes proud of us when we do well and delighted with our triumphs. If wanting the children to have the best of everything and giving priority to their happiness is not what we mean by the Fatherhood of God, what could we mean by it?

To apply the image of God's Fatherhood, quite naively, can illuminate the theological questions large and small that human beings find themselves asking. God's transcendent goodness is not an impossibly obscure mystery, if it can be compared with this familiar but special kind of human love, which transcends the reasonable goodwill that governs people's everyday dealings with one another. The ordinary friendly concern often shown by the human beings we encounter all the time does not aspire to be divine. Their kindness does not authorize imposing on them and battening on them. It would be unfair to upset them with our latest hurts and worries. But the special vocation of the parents who brought us into the world is expected to go beyond fairness. Because human creatures could not survive their long childhood without continuing devoted support, children need to make unbounded demands upon their parents and depend upon them for tireless comfort. Parental love is therefore fit to be an image of God's love.

It is not false to describe God as a Law-giver who teaches immature people the difference between right and wrong. God does indeed give laws to humanity, not capricious rules but life-enhancing principles. Looking after a family is not so much a matter of keeping them in order as of fostering their growth. The heavenly Father forbids gluttony and avarice for the same reasons as human parents forbid their children to be greedy and selfish. God commands human beings to be faithful, not to spoil their fun but because people need to be able to depend upon one another in order to become truly themselves. We may imagine God as watching longingly to see people grow up to be men and women who are capable of happiness.

30. Mark 1:15.

31. I have tried to cast doubt on the notion that God has to be "impassible," if that means that God "does not mind." See "God impassible?" under "God" in the Index.

For bringing up offspring, nourishment is more basic than commandments. It accords with the image of God the Parent to consider what nourishment is provided for the family. Christians are nurtured by food and by words, by sacraments and scripture.[32] It fits too, that for offspring to become mature is a long slow process, so that a main quality their parents need is patience and even self-restraint. The Father introduces sons and daughters to a real and strenuous world where a loving parent cannot control everything, not because of weakness, but because to keep exerting power would not be a coherent way to bring up a family. A responsible parent has to exemplify the kind of steadfastness that does not spoil the children but allows them to learn. If a Victorian father did actually say, "This hurts me more than it hurts you," he was probably not a hypocrite. He may have been inflexible and harsh, but he surely did mind.

Unanswered prayers can become less perplexing, if children of God realize that they do not know best. Someone who is asking forlornly, "Why is God taking no notice when I am begging for comfort?" might picture God as a mother who has to decide when to wean her baby.[33] Sending a child to school can look at the time only too much like forsaking, but it is the parents who will not let go of their children who are the culpable ones.

A would-be mature Christian may be inclined to disparage prayers of petition and intercession, making requests for oneself and for other people, as childish and even selfish ways to pray. The notorious recurrent problem for faith, "What is the point of petitionary prayer? Will God not give us what we need without requiring us to ask for it?" invites attention to the not trivial importance of teaching children the grace of courtesy. To say "Please" and to receive blessings, whether human or divine, with gratitude is more life-enhancing than to make a firm stand on what people claim to deserve.

Meditating, or sublimely contemplating, are more high-powered ways of entering God's presence than "I want," but when nothing seems to happen but daydreaming, it is time to go back to childish beginnings and to be encouraged by the teaching in the Gospels, and in St. Paul's epistles, that immaturity is not a barrier to finding God, and may be a stepping-stone. Children have to make a wobbly start in order to learn to walk. It is the admission that "we do not know how to pray as we ought"[34] that leads St.

32. See above, Chapter 7, 50; Chapter 10, 77; Chapter 13, 97.
33. 1 Cor 3:1–2.
34. Rom 8:26.

Paul to the resounding declaration that nothing "in all creation will be able to separate us from the love of God in Christ Jesus our Lord."[35]

Still more naively, it is well to ponder the marvelous patience of the heavenly Father, who longs to give the children everything they want but who sometimes has to endure the pain of seeing them unhappy, or even making them unhappy, for the sake of their lasting happiness that is at stake. Babies have to be weaned. Believers may have to say, "Truly, thou art a God who hidest thyself,"[36] but they can see the point, that a good parent must not try to plan all the details of the children's lives, nor even to keep them entirely protected from adversity. The omnipotent God could arrange anything, but a creation so governed would be impoverished; and worse, it would be an unreal artificial show.

God is free not to exert all the power God could exert. Christians are familiar with the idea that God the Son is all the greater because he "emptied himself"[37] and became restricted to the finite form of a human being, for the sake of humanity. Likewise they can think of God the Almighty Creator as positively holding back from controlling everything with omnipotent might, for the sake of establishing a universe in which creatures can live real lives and learn how to make real choices.

Children who are becoming adults have their own work to do, which they must be allowed and encouraged to undertake, even at hard cost to their loving parents who understand that they must not keep intervening. The author of the Epistle to the Hebrews dared to compare the Son of God himself to a child who "learnt obedience through what he suffered."[38] The Son's calling led to a destination where his Father had to refrain and withdraw, allowing the agony at Gethsemane[39] and the cry of dereliction on the Cross.[40] The image of God's Fatherhood sheds the clearest light on the awesome implications of the doctrine that God is love.[40]

35. Rom 8:39.
36. Isa 45:15.
37. Phil 2:7 (RSV).
38. Heb 5:8.
39. Matt 26:36–45; Mark 14:32–41.
40. Matt 27:46; Mark 15:34.

18

Mercy

> Yea, like as a father pitieth his own children: even
> so is the Lord merciful unto them that fear him.
>
> PSALM 103:13

THE LORD TAUGHT HIS disciples, by contrast and comparison, how to think about the Almighty Father in heaven. The image of God the King emphasizes the contrast of God's kingdom with human government.[1] The image of God the Father compares the familiar devoted love of human parents with the fatherhood of God.[2]

Both images call attention to the importance in God's sight of the insignificant or unacceptable outsiders who are easily ignored. On the one hand, God's kingdom makes room for the inadequate or wayward individuals whom earthly regimes leave to sink or swim. On the other hand, God's fatherhood can be positively likened to the tenacious partiality of human parents, who go on loving their unpromising badly-behaved offspring, seemingly against all reason.[3] Thinking kindly about unattractive people is a challenge. It helps to take hold of the idea how much each one of them matters to the heavenly Father.

---

1. E.g., Matt 5:3, 5; 8:11; 18:1–4, 19:14; Mark 9:35, 10:14–15, 23; Luke 6:20, 18:15–16, 24; John 18:36.

2. E.g., Matt 7:11; Luke 6:36; 11:11–13.

3. E.g., Luke 15:20, 22–24

Of course it often needs to be insisted that God is "no respecter of persons";[4] but sometimes it is more important to state the contrary, that God indeed does favor particular human beings, not by paying attention to some people in unfair partisanship, but by divinely valuing every individual one. The contrast between God's love and human love is not that God has no special favorites but that everyone is a special favorite. The prodigal son who is treated better than he deserves is not robbing his deserving elder brother of their father's love.[5]

A parent who is asked "Which do you love best?" may reply indignantly, "I love them all alike." A better answer would be: "I love them all differently. They are incomparable, incommensurable. They do not need to compete with one another." Only an infinite God could include more than a small number of people in such unfailing particular partiality. When Christians look fondly at their own nearest and dearest, longing to provide them straightaway with all manner of good things, they can consider that their heavenly Father minds about all of them much more still, intending the full happiness of each one. Only the heavenly Father can truly understand how excellently different the growing children are, how variegated ordinary humanity is, how many good ways of life there can be for human beings. God will judge, but God will not stereotype, fussily trying to force all the family into one pattern.

There are plenty of biblical images that shed light from different angles on what Christians believe about God's grace: the Potter who skillfully shapes the clay, the Shepherd who truly cares for the sheep, the Lamb without blemish who is sacrificed for us . . . St. John's image of the heavenly Advocate defending the prisoner in the dock[6] is often affirmed and indeed taken for granted. It is a good image for characterizing the Son of God as my Representative who is on my side, taking my part, understanding my affairs better than I do and looking for the weaknesses in my position only in order to put my case at its strongest.

It is when people fail to respond to God's grace that the major Christian image of God as the Father of the family, far from being cancelled, comes into its own. Bringing up offspring is demanding. Babies are egoists. Toddlers have tantrums. Children are heedless. Teenagers are unruly. Sometimes young people leave home and recklessly sow wild oats. The

---

4. E.g., Acts 10:34; Jas 2:1–7.

5. Luke 15:31–32.

6. E.g., 1 John 2:1.

recalcitrance of the next generation may be exhausting, infuriating, and distressing: but their parents' minding is not diminished.

Calming down, saying "sorry," arising and coming home,[7] allow the hurts to be well healed. Christians know perfectly well that Christ's teaching about the heavenly Father means this for God's whole family, but they find it hard to take it to heart and apply it to one another's faults. It is easier to insist that sinners must first pay the due price for their own misdeeds, than to realize that God's love is "full, perfect, and *sufficient.*"[8]

Well-behaved people realize, sometimes too clearly, that moral values require principled firmness, not fond leniency. They understand that it is not good enough to have a soft spot for endearing delinquents. If God the Father's generous mercy meant condoning the harm the children do and saying indulgently, "Never mind," how could the verdict of God the Judge be anything but "Guilty"? Sins have consequences; and damage demands redress. The Lord heard the blood of murdered Abel crying out from the ground.[9] Even a divine judge cannot have the right to bypass the wrongs of victims, kindly pardoning without more ado the offenses perpetrated by their enemies.[10]

How can God's justice permit mercy for sinners? The "penal theory" of the Atonement is the answer that is provided by Christian moralists who heed the gravity of sin. They declare that justice is satisfied and wrongdoers can be forgiven, because the price has been paid. The Son of God has propitiated the Father's wrath by accepting the punishment we deserve. For many traditional Christians, that statement sums up the gospel. They do not take it as just one possible suggestion about what God's mercy to sinners means. They affirm this price-paying as the heart of the good news. For others, this "penal theory," which insists that somebody must be punished in the name of justice, even the wrong person, is a travesty of divine forgiveness, positing a vengeful, unmerciful, and unfair God.

If the deliverance of sinners meant that the Advocate pleaded guilty and was convicted instead of the accused, the Atonement would collapse into romantic injustice. When instead the emphasis is put on the image of God as Father, not giving judgment in a court but bringing up a family, God's mercy is no less needful and no less momentous; but it does not have

---

7. Luke 15:18.

8. *The Book of Common Prayer*, Holy Communion, Prayer of Consecration.

9. Gen 4:10.

10. See Oppenheimer, *On Being Someone,* 182.

to be a legal bargain negotiated between a stern Judge and a kind-hearted Redeemer. The Creator and the Savior are one God,[11] who has one purpose, to generate and perfect a world full of people, whatever pains it takes.

The comparison of the love of God for human beings with the love of a good parent is indeed an encouraging doctrine. It is not therefore a doctrine of glib optimism that takes no notice when things go wrong. If God can be pleased, God can be sorry and even hurt. The children's troubles are a trouble to their Father, their debts are a burden and their faults are a sorrow. They are safe because God is in charge, unshaken and unworried, but not untouched.[12]

The Christian doctrine of Atonement needs, not exactly a penal theory, but a *cost* theory. Punishments are not always the best response to offenses. Sins can be forgiven and set aside; *but* the damage is still real and has to be borne. Justice is not done if a comfortable onlooker ignores the wrong and offers a capricious free pardon to the culprits. Forgiving other people's enemies is presumptuous. Christians should not affirm unthinkingly that God, and God alone, can forgive sinners. How can God forgive at all, from heaven above? It takes a victim to forgo revenge and generously restore the wrongdoers. The divine Victim who suffered under Pontius Pilate experienced at first hand the harm that human beings do and therefore had real wrongs of his own to forgive. There is no need to say, "It was all very well for him."

Christians who call God Father dare to state, not as a legal fiction but as a moral reality, that God is not detached from human life but takes responsibility for what happens in God's universe.[13] Parents are answerable to their children for bringing them into this troubled world; and they are accountable to other people when their growing children have done damage. They have undertaken these liabilities and they carry this burden. If Christians speak in this way about God's responsibility for humanity, they are not being presumptuous but attending to the teaching of the New Testament. For the mercy of God to overcome, not condone, what had gone wrong, it was necessary for the Creator to become vulnerable and suffer alongside suffering creatures; to face death as they must, and then to rise again as God's pledge that death is defeated.[14]

11. John 10:30; 2 Cor 5:19.

12. See 136n31 above.

13. See "God's responsibility" under "God" in the Index.

14. E.g., Matt 16:21; Mark 8:31; Luke 9:22, 24:25–26; Acts 3:15.

Because Christians believe that Jesus Christ is God the Son, God with us,[15] they can believe on his authority the extravagantly hopeful message that God the Father loves the children through thick and thin, even when they ungratefully misbehave. They accordingly proclaim that God's love is *unconditional*. This declaration could actually be misleading, if "unconditional" meant "automatic." For the Father's love to reach the children, there are in a way two conditions after all, or rather requirements. These are not stipulations that proper procedures must be carried out to earn God's mercy. They are indications of the frame of mind in which anyone could actually receive it.

The first requirement, repentance, is indeed plainly specified in the Gospels. God offers mercy to sinful human beings, but an impenitent sinner is shut in a place where mercy cannot take hold, because the way in is blocked from the human side. To realize that one has behaved badly but still fail to be sorry is to take oneself out of reach. The encouragement shown to Julian of Norwich was the assurance that there is no barrier on God's side. "I truly saw that he was willing to die as often as he was able to die, and love would never let him rest until he had done it."[16] "'Look how much I loved you'. Our good Lord revealed this to make us glad and joyful."[17]

When Simon Peter for all his protestations lost his courage and denied his loyalty, his failure came home to him when the cock crowed and the Lord turned and looked at him. "And he went out and wept bitterly."[18] The admission of human defeat provides the foothold for divine mercy. When the Lord had suffered death and had risen, the next installment of Saint Peter's story is the resurrection of his calling to be an apostle, which is described in the Fourth Gospel[19] but indicated most tellingly in Mark's account of the angels' message to the women at the tomb. "But go, tell his disciples *and Peter* that he is going before you to Galilee; there you will see him, as he told you."[20]

To be sorry and to want mercy is the first requirement for letting God's grace come through. The second is simply not to set up obstacles, especially not to block the way by refusing mercy to fellow offenders. An unforgiving

15. Matt 1:23; Matt 16:15–16; Mark 8:29; Luke 9:20.

16. Julian of Norwich, *Revelations of Divine Love*, Chapter 24.

17. Ibid., Chapters 22 and 24.

18. Luke 22:60–62; Matt 26:75; Mark 14:72–73.

19. John 21:3, 7, 15–19.

20. Mark 16:7.

sinner, however remorseful, has missed the point and failed to grasp what restoration means. The Gospels emphatically reiterate the teaching of Jesus that merciless people are incapable of receiving mercy.[21] Human beings can exclude themselves from their Father's kindness.

Many people of goodwill have been desperately troubled by a reported saying of Jesus that God's mercy is not infinite after all, but quite strictly limited. Though all manner of sins and blasphemies will be forgiven to human beings, "whoever blasphemes against the Holy Spirit never has forgiveness, but is guilty of an eternal sin."[22] "There is a sin against Him which damns you for ever," said Dorothy L. Sayers, "but nobody knows what it is."[23]

Committed disciples and hostile antagonists, and uncommitted critics, are all apt to take hard sayings out of context, using them as proof-texts to confirm hasty judgments, for or against belief. More skeptically minded inquirers and opponents are inclined to withhold assent and to treat difficult pronouncements as, so-to-say, disproof-texts. Finding the offered lessons unacceptable, they sadly or scornfully reject the Teacher.

The hard saying about the sin against the Holy Spirit can be put back in its context. People were dismissing the works of healing, which they could see Jesus doing among them, not recognizing them as good works but calling them the work of the devil. It appears that the deadly sin is to identify as evil what is evidently good, perversely shutting out accessible enlightenment. "How great is that darkness."[24] It is spiritual suicide to repudiate the *inspiration* of the Holy *Spirit*, who is God present within us enlightening us.[25] God's mercy is not impeded by divine unmerciful severity, but by human hard-heartedness that sets up a barrier fatally immovable from outside.

But still we cannot judge the state of one another's souls and be confident about anyone's condemnation. In the light of the whole gospel, Christians must not happily accept, as the full meaning of this difficult saying, that because a sinner who is actually shutting out God's mercy is committing an offense that pardon cannot reach, that sinner must evidently be divinely fixed in the present tense, blaspheming for ever, permanently unforgivable. Christians may hope, and indeed pray, that the inexorable

---

21. E.g., Matt 5:7; 6:12, 14–15; 18:23–35; Mark 11:26; Luke 6:37.

22. Mark 3:28–30.

23. Sayers, *Creed or Chaos?*, 22.

24. Matt 6:23.

25. See above, Chapter 9, 70; Chapter 13, 96, 100.

judgment which will never condone hard-heartedness does not decree that a heart which has been hard will remain forever unsoftened, ineligible for resurrection. The other saying still stands, that there will be joy in heaven over one sinner who repents.[26]

The image of God as Father of the human family stands out as more significant than an attractive embellishment to the gospel story, a vivid way of expressing the faith that God has mercy on human beings and instructs them to have mercy on one another. The image is at the center of Christian belief, because it puts mercy for God's children in place as neither trivial nor out of reach.

When serious wrong has been done, forgiveness is momentous. People who care about goodness understandably think that letting offenders go unpunished cannot even be allowable, because leniency is unjust not admirable. Taking clemency for granted and saying easily "You are forgiven" suggests failure to understand the problem. Pious Christians who react by offering knee-jerk pardon, in God's name, when confronted by major damage look uncaring and even hypocritical. "It's all very well to announce that God forgives: he's not the injured party."

But if God is rightly compared with the father of the human family, the mercy of God is not the easy tolerance of a fairly unconcerned stranger. Parents forgive their children, naturally but not casually, because what they care for is the children's well-being. If it is true that human beings are siblings, the forbearance they show towards God's other children's failings, for their Father's sake, springs from their family feeling, which is neither culpable nor heroic.

When parents forgive their child, or husband and wives back each other through thick and thin, or when brothers and sisters close their ranks to protect a beloved black sheep, their loyalty is natural and appropriate rather than irresponsible. These people are part of each other's lives and can be expected to go on minding about each other, or at least to put up with each other, rather than hurt the whole family.

When children are growing up together, at least their petty grievances are "easily borne,"[27] not dire. One day they may have to face adult wrongs, when it seems that nothing can ever be the same again. Rather than gritting one's teeth and hoping to forget, it is more promising to say, "I can't feel the old affection for him any more, but he is still my parents' child and

26. Luke 15:7.

27. Browning, "After," *Poems,* vol. 1, 651.

of course they love him." When St. Stephen was being stoned he did not pronounce on his own authority, "I forgive them" but prayed "Lord, do not hold this sin against them,"[28] calling on the name of the Lord Jesus, who had committed his own killers to his Father's mercy rather than to his Father's vengeance.[29]

If the enemies of the Son of God had known what they were doing, whom they were hurting and trying to destroy, then the sin of which they needed to repent, in order to receive God's forgiveness, would have been blasphemy. Perhaps the gap between human and divine offense is not so great. If indeed every sin against any of God's seemingly insignificant children matters to their Father, every unkindness to one another will turn out to have been an affront to our Maker, not trivial but profoundly hurtful, needing supernatural mercy.

28. Acts 7:60.

29. Luke 23:34.

19

Continuing

And they continued steadfastly in the apostles'
doctrine and fellowship, and in breaking of bread,
and in prayers.

ACTS 2:42

THE CHRISTIAN FAITH IS based on the conviction that the universe
did not merely happen, but was created on purpose and was worth
creating. The image of God the Maker, who commanded the world to come
into being,[1] comes before the images of King or Father. "And God said,
'let there be light'; and there was light. And God saw that the light was
good."[2] Believers are committed all along to the faith that the universe is
a magnificent work, not an accident, still less a disaster. They affirm that
nature, including humanity, is not a product of impersonal chance, nor of
irresponsible divine doodling, but is indeed a divine work of art.

"And God saw everything that he had made, and behold, it was very
good."[3] The worthwhileness of God's whole creation underlies the Christian
conviction that each person in the world, including everyone's own self, is
infinitely valuable. It is no credit to our Maker if creatures are written off as
substandard. Most people matter to somebody, even if only to themselves.
Christians believe that human beings really are as important in God's eyes

1. Gen 1:1; Ps 33:9.

2. Gen 1:3–4.

3. Gen 1:4, 10, 12, 18, 21, 25, 31.

as they seem to be to whoever loves them most. They are worth all the trouble they give. Faith looks beyond the undeniable sinfulness of humanity to find God's grace.

The paradox of atonement is that the mercy of God, which meets and overcomes evil, turns out not to be merely a second best expedient, as if uneventful stability would have been better.[4] The history of the world has been enhanced, indeed crowned, by God's generosity, for which sin has been the occasion. "O felix culpa"—"O happy fault, which has earned such a mighty Redeemer."[5]

The story that starts with God's creation and leads to God's coming into the world has taken shape as a story that plunged into tragedy, twisted out of a graceful shape at the start. The Creator's purpose to make a world of blessed creatures has never been a joy-ride and has proved to be a difficult and arduous enterprise. Evidently there have been tribulations in the universe all along, before the first men and women arrived, since one cannot suppose that no suffering but human suffering matters.[6] It is impossible now to dismiss the long processes of evolution that gave rise to sentient animals and eventually to people. The first chapters of the Book of Genesis are inspired poetry, compressing the huge work of the Maker of the universe into six days. They are not historical information about a particular prehistoric date, when a mature man and woman were formed out of the dust of the earth and began forthwith to spoil the excellence of the garden of Eden by disobedience.

Christians have to try to understand why the creation had to be so problematical. They can see reasons connected with depth rather than shallowness, suggesting that victory after struggles is more finally satisfying than unbroken ease.[7] Edwin Muir doubted whether hope and pity could ever have blossomed in Eden.[8] The dangerous complexities of this world are needed to allow some wonderful blessings to take root and flower.

God evidently refrains from arranging every detail of history and has therefore permitted a real risk of happenings that are contrary to God's will.[9] The risk has materialized. Christians who are too sophisticated to

4. See above, Chapter 4, 32; Chapter 11, 84.

5. The Missal, "Exultet" on Holy Saturday.

6. See above, Chapter 4, 27; Chapter 5, 36.

7. See note 4 above and Oppenheimer, Making Good, e.g., 103, 121.

8. Muir, "One Foot in Eden," Collected Poems. See above, Chapter 4, 32 and note 10 there.

9. See above, Chapter 5, 35, 37; Chapter 11, 83f.

be comfortably convinced that a fiendish enemy with cloven hooves set about wreaking all the harm,[10] and who cannot believe that it was the first two human beings who did all the damage, must ascribe the heavy weight of natural evils to the workings of chance, not arranged but allowed by the Creator.[11] People who go on believing in the goodness of God need the two provisos:[12] that God bears the responsibility; and that the final upshot will be recognizable as a glorious triumph.

Human beings find themselves living in an interim time, in which the travailing of creation[13] makes faith in God look desperately hard and even apparently impossible. Excellence and damage are mixed. Evidently even the wisest human beings cannot see the whole picture, which in any case is not yet complete. Nature is a work in progress. God's kingdom is still to be established. God the Father is bringing up the growing children.

Christians have to realize how human sins keep contributing to the troubled story, so that happy reverence and gratitude to God our Creator are submerged in the darker obligations of sombre reverence and gratitude to God our Saviour. What is required of would-be disciples is not hasty optimism but willingness to respond, in God's name, to what they have seen so far, hoping to be shown more: like St. Paul, who did not count himself to have apprehended but pressed on towards the prize.[14]

Neither skepticism not credulity is a virtue. A somewhat argumentative Christian, who finds skepticism more tempting than credulity, who cannot claim to know the answers by intuition, is bound to rely upon reasoning in order to find out truth. An important aspect of pressing on towards the prize is *thinking*, using whatever intellectual powers one has been given in order to understand more. Reasoning is one kind of moral behaving. Some of us have the duty to study the available data, in order to see the picture better and to tell one another what we can see. The aim is not to illuminate reality with light of one's own, but to open the shutters to let in whatever light is coming from outside, and to look attentively at what the daylight shows. We set out our findings, not to rest in a task completed, but as a convenient consolidation of progress so far. We take stock of where we are, not to stop but to go on.

10. Matt 13:25–28.

11. See Note 9 above; and Chapter 5:38.

12. See above, Chapter 5:37f.

13. Rom 8:22.

14. Phil 3:13–14.

Thinking Christians need not do their reasoning in isolation from others, any more than Christians who find simple faith easy have to serve God all by themselves. People who cannot take belief in God for granted, who have adopted it as a hypothesis that needs experimental testing,[15] can test it best by participating in Christian living, so as to find out what turns out to make sense. One learns, like pupils in a school or colleagues in a project, from the experience of responsible people.

"You must have faith" ought not to mean, "Squash your doubts" but "Taste and see."[16] When people find nourishment that they could not have provided for themselves, they may be able to recognize God's active presence. There is no proof here to convince critics that Christianity is true; but there is reassurance for hopeful believers, that they need not succumb to the taunt that their faith is ungrounded nonsense.[17] They can set out to follow the way, looking for confirmation as they go along that they are on the right road.

As a Christian who holds that thinking and communicating are important duties of human creatures, I am bound to report what I have myself received and submit it to the judgment of other people. Though I cannot prove my faith, I did not invent it. I was taught it, mostly but perhaps not exclusively, by other Christians. Of course I am thinking wishfully: I urgently want the Christian faith to be true. But I am not thinking fancifully: I take heed of the evidence. Full verification awaits the fulfillment of the kingdom of heaven, but in the meantime it is responsible behavior to entrust one's life to this hypothesis, in the same sort of way as people responsibly ride bicycles. They have seen people do it, and they can find out how to do it themselves, not by saying "Of course it's impossible to balance on two wheels," but by learning how to get up some momentum.

The strong support for the Christian hypothesis that the universe was created is the recorded experience of the people of God through centuries, culminating in the gospel of Christ. The story offers glimpses of a great and holy God, who has turned out to be more complex than one simple divine Power. God has been made known in history as a Trinity of three Persons, the Father, the Son and the Holy Spirit. "The Father" is the plainest image of God's nature, indicating Somebody who brought us into existence, loves us for our own sake and intends our complete happiness. "The Son" is our

15. See above, Chapter 7, 47–48.

16. Ps 34:8.

17. See above, Chapter 6, 42.

image of God in action, God alongside us, coming at a particular time and bearing the brunt of what human life is like. "The Holy Spirit" signifies God within us, communicating with human beings in all times and places, sometimes by subtle hints, sometimes more plainly.[18]

Without expecting to hold conversations with the Almighty, I can believe that the Holy Spirit is most likely to reveal God's reality to me by inspiring my thoughts, putting ideas into my head. Austin Farrer's account of his experience makes sense,[19] that although he could not find God appearing to him face-to-face, his thinking would sometimes become "diaphanous," giving him recognizable glimpses of the source of the light, especially when he tried to think about God.

I can gratefully apply this image of God's presence by using the prayer, "God be in my head."[20] I might reverse two of its clauses: "God be in my head: *and in my thinking*" and "God be in my heart: *and in my understanding*." That way round, the prayer begins by asking God to be present in the place where I characteristically start. Then it can bring to mind the story of King Solomon,[21] who pleased the Lord by not asking for divine providence to arrange his flourishing, but by praying for "a wise and understanding heart," the gift of discernment.

A believer who is glad to use ancient words to ask for God's blessing can be particularly glad to go on to the end of the prayer, "God be at mine end; and at my departing," begging for grace not to be afraid of the unknown future which all human beings face. It is not true that a good Christian will be untroubled by the "Arch Fear" of death.[22] Robert Browning knew that "the strong man must go."[23] Few people can leave "the warm precincts of the cheerful day" without casting "one longing lingering look behind."[24]

It is all very well to preach oneself sermons: "You must have faith"; or to produce debating points, like Shakespeare's Julius Caesar, bravely but illogically announcing, on what turns out to be the day of his assassination, that death is simply not fearful, because it "will come when it will

18. See above, Chapter 13, 96n5; Chapter 17, 132.

19. See above, Chapter 13, 100.

20. See above, ibid.

21. 1 Kgs 3:5–14.

22. Robert Browning "Prospice," *Poetical Works.*

23. Ibid.

24. Gray, "Elegy Written in a Country Churchyard."

come."[25] Claudio in *Measure for Measure* is more human when he begs his sister to sacrifice her virtue for his life, terrified "to die, and go we know not where."[26] If worry gets a hold, it is an affliction particularly hard to overcome, whether it appears as timid alarm, wild panic, cosmic doubt, or nagging fretfulness wrecking everyday contentment. The Gospels indeed take anxiety more seriously as contrary to Christian faith than the sins of the flesh. To acknowledge one's human fears and hand them over for God to manage is a better antidote than trying to conquer them by willpower.

What assurance is there that God can overcome fear? To pray, "God be at mine end; and at my departing" is to ask God to be present, keeping us company, which is indeed what the gospel of Christ's coming does promise. "His name shall be called Emmanuel, which means, God with us."[27] A Christian does not have to step alone into the future. The Lord has been here and experienced the full range of well-founded horror and dismay,[28] before the dawning hope of the Easter dénouement appeared, when "on the first day of the week Mary Magdalen came to the tomb early, while it was still dark, and saw that the stone had been taken away from the tomb":[29] The good news of the real presence of God in human life depends upon both the dreadful Cross and the triumphant Rising.

To set about telling the truth about life and death as far as I can understand it, I can explore different imagery, fanciful or traditional, like the householder who brings out of his treasure things new and old.[30] When I imagine myself as a goldfish who cannot see out of the aquarium, I dare to believe that at last I will be adopted by a more venerable fish. The Greek *ichthus* has been used as a Christian symbol since early days, because its letters, I, X, Th, Y, S, stand for the initials of the Christian hope, Jesus Christ, God's Son, Savior.[31]

ΙΧΘΥΣ

25. *Julius Caesar*, II, 2, 32–37.

26. *Measure for Measure*, III, 1.

27. Matt 1:23.

28. Matt 26:32; Mark 14:33; Luke 22:43.

29. John 20:1.

30. Matt 13:52. See above, Chapter 1, 4.

31. Cross and Livingstone, eds., *Oxford Dictionary of the Christian Church*, 613.

Bibliography

This is not a list of further reading, but an attempt to indicate where people so minded could follow up my references. I have given a few dates, especially for ancient and medieval authors. I have put the books of the Bible and the plays of Shakespeare in the Index, rather than including them here.

Abelard, Peter (1079–1142). "O Quanta Qualia." No. 349 in *The Oxford Hymn Book*. Oxford: Oxford University Press, 1908.

Arnold, Matthew. *Poems*. Oxford: Oxford University Press, 1909.

Augustine. *Confessions* (354–430). Translated by Henry Chadwick. Oxford: Oxford University Press, 1991.

———. *Select Letters*. Translated by J. H. Baxter. London: Heinemann, 1930.

Barr, James. *The Bible in the Modern World*. London: SCM, 1972

———. *Escaping from Fundamentalism*. London, SCM, 1984.

———. *Fundamentalism*. London: SCM, 1977.

Bauckham, Richard. *Jesus: A Very Short Introduction*. Oxford: Oxford University Press, 2011.

———. *Jesus and the Eyewitnesses: The Gospels as Eyewitness Testimony*. Grand Rapids: Eerdmans 2006.

Book of Common Prayer (1662). Oxford: Oxford University Press, n.d.

Broad, C. D. *The Mind and Its Place in Nature*. London: Kegan Paul, 1925.

———. *Knowledge and Belief*. Oxford: Oxford University Press, 1959.

Browning, Robert. *Poems*. Harmondsworth, England: Penguin, 1981.

Buford, T., ed. *Essays on Other Minds*. Champaign, IL: University of Illinois Press, 1970.

Burns, Robert. "O My Luve's Like a Red, Red Rose." In *The Golden Treasury of the Best Songs and Lyrical Poems in the English Language,"* edited by Francis Turner Palgrave, 150. Oxford: Oxford University Press, 1996.

Butler, Joseph (1692–1752). *The Works of Joseph Butler*, 3 vols. Edited by W. E. Gladstone. Oxford: Clarendon, 1896.

de Chardin, Pierre Teilhard. *Le milieu divin*, 1957. English translation, *The Divine Milieu*. London: Collins, 1960

Coleman, Peter. "Is Religion the Friend of Ageing?" Third Leveson Lecture, 2004. Published as Leveson Paper 9 by the Leveson Centre for the Study of Ageing, Spirituality and Social Policy, Temple Balsall, Birmingham.

Bibliography

Cross, F. L., and E. A. Livingstone, eds. *Oxford Dictionary of the Christian Church,* 3rd ed. Oxford: Oxford University Press, 1997.

Dante Alighieri (1265–1321). *Divina Commedia.* London: J. M. Dent & Sons, 1900, with English translation.

Descartes, Réné (1546–1659). *Discourse on Method.* Translated by Ian Maclean. Oxford: Oxford University Press, 2006.

Dunn, James. *Beginning from Jerusalem.* Grand Rapids: Eerdmans, 2009

———. *Jesus Remembered.* Grand Rapids: Eerdmans, 2003.

———. *The Living Word.* London: SCM, 1987.

Farrer, Austin. *A Celebration of Faith.* London: Hodder & Stoughton, 1970.

———. *Eucharistic Theology Then and Now.* SPCK Theological Collections 9. London: SPCK, 1968.

———. *The Glass of Vision.* The Bampton Lectures for 1948. London: Dacre, 1948.

———. *A Science of God?* London: Bles, 1966.

Gibbon, Edward. *Decline and Fall of the Roman Empire,* 7 vol. Edited with notes by J. B. Bury. London: Methuen, 1926.

Gray, Thomas. "Elegy written in a Country Churchyard." (1751) In *The Golden Treasury of the Best Songs and Lyrical Poems in the English Language,"* edited by Francis Turner Palgrave, 145. Oxford: Oxford University Press, 1996.

Gregory of Nyssa (331–395). *The Life of Moses.* Classics of Western Spirituality. Mahwah, NJ: Paulist, 1978.

Hart, H. L. A. *The Concept of Law.* Oxford Clarendon Law Series. Oxford: Clarendon, 1961.

Hume, David. "Of Miracles." In *Enquiry Concerning the Human Understanding,* 2nd ed., edited by L. A. Selby-Bigge, 109–31. Oxford: Clarendon, 1902.

Julian of Norwich (c.1342– after 1413). *Revelations of Divine Love.* Classics of Western Spirituality. Mahwah, NJ: Paulist, 1978.

Kant, Immanuel. *Critique of Practical Reason.* New York: Classic Books International, 2010.

Lewis, C. S. *The Screwtape Letters and Screwtape Proposes a Toast.* London: Bles,1961.

Lowell, James R. "Once to Every Man and Nation." First published in *The Boston Courier,* November 12, 1845.

Macaulay, Lord. *Works.* Vol. VIII. London: Longmans, Green & Co., 1875.

Mitchell, Basil. *The Justification of Religious Belief.* New York: Macmillan, 1973.

Moule, C. F. D. *Christ Alive and at Large.* Edited and introduced by Robert Morgan and Patrick Moule. Canterbury Studies in Spiritual Theology. London: Canterbury, 2010.

Muir, Edwin. *Collected Poems 1921–1958.* London: Faber & Faber, 1960.

Murdoch, Iris. *The Sovereignty of Good.* London: Routledge, 1970.

Oppenheimer, Helen. "The Experience of Aging." *Concilium* (June 1991) 39–45.

———. Fourth Leveson Lecture at Temple Walsall, Birmingham. "The Experience of Aging: A Challenge to Christian Belief." Published as Leveson Paper 11, 2005, by the Leveson Centre for the Study of Ageing, Spirituality and Social Policy.

———. *Helping Children Find God.* Harrisburg, PA: Morehouse, 1994. Published in the UK as *Finding and Following: Talking with Children about God.* London: SCM, 1994.

———. *The Hope of Happiness.* London: SCM, 1983.

———. *The Hope of Heaven: What Happens When We Die?* Cambridge, MA: Cowley, 1988. Published in the UK as *Looking Before and After.* Glasgow: Fount, 1988.

———. *Incarnation and Immanence.* London: Hodder & Stoughton, 1973.

————. *Making Good.* London: SCM, 2001

————. *Marriage. Ethics: Our Choices.* London: Mowbrays, 1990.

————. *On Being Someone.* Exeter: Imprint Academic, 2011.

————. *What a Piece of Work: On Being Human.* Exeter UK and Charlottesville, VA USA: Imprint Academic, 2006.

Plato (c.428–348 B.C). *Euthyphro Dialogue.* Edited by John Burnet. Oxford: Clarendon, 1977.

Platten, Stephen. "Reanimating Sacrifice." *Theology* January/February 2012, 26–35.

Plotinus (c.205–270). *Enneads.* Loeb Classical Library. Cambridge, MA: Harvard University Press, 1989.

Polkinghorne, John. *Science and Providence.* West Conshohocken, PA: Templeton Foundation, 2005.

Price, H. H. *Belief.* Sydney: Allen & Unwin, 1969.

————. *Perception.* London: Methuen, 1932.

Rowell, Geoffrey, Kenneth Stevenson, and Rowan Williams, eds. *Love's Redeeming Work: The Anglican Quest for Holiness.* Oxford: Oxford University Press, 2001.

Russell, Bertrand. *The Problems of Philosophy.* Oxford: Oxford University Press, 1979.

Ryle, Gilbert. *The Concept of Mind.* London: Hutchinson, 1949

Saint Simon, Duc de (1675–1755). *Historical Memoirs: A Shortened Version.* Edited and translated by Lucy Norton. London: Hamish Hamilton, 1968.

Saki (H. H. Munro). "Reginald at the Theatre." *The Short Stories of Saki.* London: The Bodley Head Ltd, 1930.

Sartre, Jean-Paul. *Huis Clos.* English translation *No Exit.* London: Methuen, 1987.

Sayers, Dorothy L. *The Nine Tailors.* London: Victor Gollancz, 1934.

————. *Creed or Chaos?* London: Methuen, 1947.

Shand, John. "A Refutation of the Existence of God." *Think: A Journal of the Royal Institute of Philosophy* 26:9 (Autumn 2010) 61–79.

Shaw, G. B. "Preface to *Androcles and the Lion.*" In *Collected Plays with Their Prefaces,* vol. IV. London: The Bodley Head, 1972.

Tennyson, Alfred, Lord. *The Poems of Tennyson,* 3 vols., 2nd ed. Harlow: Longmans, 1987.

Traherne, Thomas (c.1636–1674). *Centuries, Poems, and Thanksgivings. 2 vols.* Clarendon Press: Oxford, Clarendon, 1958.

Vanstone W. H. *Love's Endeavour, Love's Expense: The Response of Being to the Love of God.* London: Darton, Longman & Todd, 1977.

Watts, Isaac. "Against Quarrelling." In *Divine and Moral Songs for the Use of Children.* Charleston, SC: Forgotten Books, 2012.

Wordsworth, William. *Poetical Works,* 5 vols. Edited by E. de Selincourt and Helen Darbishire. Oxford: Clarendon, 1949.

Names Index

Abel 141

Abelard, Peter, "O quanta qualia," 38

Abraham, 34

Abraham, Isaac and Jacob, 16, 118

Achilles, see Tennyson

Acts of the Apostles, 55, 60, 70, 86, 96, 110, 113, 125, 140, 142, 146, 147

Adam & Eve, 27, 44, 98

Agincourt, 31

Alzheimer, 8

Andersen, Hans Christian, "The Emperor's New Clothes," 42

Arnold, Matthew, "Dover Beach," 75

Athanasian Creed, 87

As You Like It, see Shakespeare

Augustine of Hippo, *Confessions,* 82, 102, 106, 113

   Epistles, 63

Austen, Jane, 7

   Pride and Prejudice, 44

Barr, James, 73, 78

Bauckham, Richard, 44, 80, 130

Berkeley, George, 51

Bible, trustworthiness, 42–46, 73, 77–79, 80, 102; Word of God, 44, 77f, 97

Blougram, Bishop, see Browning, Robert

Broad, C. D., *The Mind and Its Place in Nature,* 42, 51

Browning, Elizabeth Barrett, 9

Browning, Robert,
   "Abt Vogler," 92

"After," 18, 145

"Bishop Blougram's Apology," 49, 52, 61

"Rabbi Ben Ezra," 9

"Prospice," 151

Buford, T., (ed.) *Essays on Other Minds* 51

Burns, Robert, 43

Butler, Joseph, *Letters,* 17

Cana of Galilee, see Jesus Christ

Clovis, 49

Coleman, Peter, "Is Religion the Friend of Aging?," 7, 89

Book of Common Prayer:
   Creeds, 47, 87
   Communion: Prayer of Consecration, 141, post-Communion, 109
   Thanksgivings, 84, 85, 110
   Catechism, 105
   Thirty-nine Articles, 87

Common Worship, 47, 109, 124

Corinthians, 1 & 2, see Paul

Daniel, 23

Dante Alighieri, 114

Darwin, Charles, 15, 27

David's Son, see Jesus Christ

Dawkins, Richard (and the new atheists), 78

Descartes, René, 51, 74, 76

Desdemona, 58

Dunn, James, 44, 65, 78, 80, 93

Eden, 32,148
Einstein, Albert, 68
Egypt, 35, 118
Elijah, 84
Elizabeth I, 44
Emmanuel, God with us, see Jesus
	Christ
Exodus 118
Eucharist, 102, 103, 106–10; see Jesus
	Christ, Last Supper
Euthyphro dialogue, see Plato
Ezekiel, 69

Farrer, Austin, 53, 100, 108, 113, 118
Father Christmas, see Santa Claus

Galilee, see Jesus Christ
Genesis: creation - of universe, 32, 70,
	79, 89, 97, 115, 134, 147;
	- of animals, 78;
	- of people, 36, 64, 115;
	myth, 80, 148
	see Adam and Eve, Abel, Abraham,
	Eden.
Gethsemane, see Jesus Christ
Gibbon, Edward, *Decline and Fall of
	the Roman Empire,* 49
Gladstone, W. E., 8 (and Butler, Jo-
	seph, in Bibliography)
Glendower, Owen, 40
God, Father, 100, 102, 121, 129–33,
	134, 139, 143, 150–51
	Son, see Jesus Christ
	Holy Spirit, 16, 50, 69, 96, 100, 102,
		104, 117, 144, 150–51
	Holy Trinity, Preface, 16, 69, 150
	God impassible? 35, 38, 59, 61,
		62–63, 64, 68, 84 (& note 9),
		87, 88, 136n31, 137, 138, 140,
		142
	God taking responsibility, 23, 33,
		34, 37, 39, 60, 63, 86, 114, 134,
		140, 141f
	"God be in my head," 100, 151
Gospels, see Bible, trustworthiness
Thomas Gray, *Elegy Written in a
	Country Churchyard,* 133, 151
Gregory of Nyssa, 93

Hamlet, see Shakespeare
Henry IV Part I, see Shakespeare
Henry V, see Shakespeare
Hebrews, Epistle, 76, 94, 98, 117, 138
Hart, H. L. A, *The Concept of Law,* 115
Hermes, 96
Horatius, see Macaulay
Hotspur, 40
Hume, David, 51, 66–67, 90, 86

Iago, 58
Isaiah, 76, 87, 96, 98, 118, 129
	Second Isaiah 133, 138
Islam, Muslims, 18

James & John, apostles, 56–57
James, Epistle, 140
Jerusalem, Council of, 125
Jesus Christ:
	Nativity, 45–46, 85, 97; Baby Jesus,
		6
	"Who is this?" 67
	Emmanuel, God with us, 67, 85,
		97, 143, 152
	Son of David, 45
	Son of man, 13; learning hu-
		manly, 63, 76, 138; tempta-
		tion, 63
	Son of God, 63, 99, 138, 151, 152
	The Way, the Truth and the Life,
		55
	Word of God, Logos, 97
	Galilee, 57, 96, 104, 108, 110, 136,
		143
	Cana of Galilee, wedding, 43, 104
Teaching:
	Father—see God the Father
	Kingdom, 92, 93, 104, 121,
		129–30, 139, 149, 150
	faith, 28, 54, 56, 58, 85–86, 90,
		132
		worry, 30, 152
	hard sayings, 44, 121, 144
	liberal or traditional? 5, 14, 41, 44,
		93, 104, 106, 117, 122, 123
	outsiders, 41; risk, 54, 123–24;
		Sabbath, 28, 44, 122; family
		life, 135

Lord's Prayer, 129
rebirth, 93–94
repentance, 136, 143, 145, 146
stories and images, 64, 121, 129
   tares, 35; pearl, 54; count the
      cost, 57; mother hen,
      64; rain, 83, 86; harvest,
      90; neighbor, 92, 97 n.8;
      prodigal son, 140
  welcome, 41
    feasting, 93; see Eucharist
Last Supper, 107–8
Passion:
  Cross, 63, 65, 88, 99, 110, 123,
    138, 152
  Gethsemane, 88, 138
  Resurrection, Rising, 57, 63, 65, 90,
    108, 119, 123, 142, 152
Job, 27, 47, 77
John, apostle, 41, 56–57
John, First Epistle, 101, 140
John of Gaunt, 7
Jonah, 41
Joseph of Nazareth, 45
Joshua, 123
Jude, Epistle, 55
Julian of Norwich, 12, 17, 18, 133,
    135, 143
Julius Caesar, see Shakespeare

Kant, Immanuel, 50
Keats, John, 5
I Kings, 84, 151

Lewis, C. S., *The Screwtape Letters,* 10,
    19, 20, 30
Leveson Lectures, Oppenheimer, 3,
    26; Coleman, 7, 89
Lindsay of Balliol, 23n5
Locke, John, 51
London, 42
Lord's Prayer, see Jesus Christ,
    teaching
Lowell, James R., 124
Luther, Martin, 103

Macaulay, T. B., Lord Macaulay,
    "Horatius," 31

Macbeth, see Shakespeare
Mary Magdalen, 152
Mary the Virgin, 45
Measure for Measure, see Shakespeare
Missal, Roman, 148
Micah, 134
Mitchell, Basil, *The Justification of
    Religious Belief,* 76
Moses, 118, 120
Moule, C. D. F., *Christ Alive and at
    Large,* 78
Muir, Edwin, "One Foot in Eden," 32,
    148
Munro, H. H., see Saki
Murdoch, Iris, *The Sovereignty of
    Good,* 48
Muslims, see Islam

Neanderthalis, homo sapiens, 14
Nebuchadnezzar, see Shadrach, Me-
    shach & Abednego
Newton, Isaac, 68
Nicene Creed, 47, 87
Nicholas of Bari, see Santa Claus

Odin, 44
Odysseus, 44; and see Tennyson,
    "Ulysses"
Oppenheimer, Helen, Bibliography
    154–55
  Concilium June 1991 "The Experi-
    ence of Aging," 3
  Helping Children Find God, 43, 61,
    68, 97, 100, 103, 105
  The Hope of Heaven, 65, 90, 93
  Incarnation and Immanence, 82, 96
  Leveson Lecture, 3, 26
  Making Good, 19, 20, 22, 23, 26, 32,
    36, 84, 87, 92, 94, 148
  Marriage, 115
  "O quanta qualia," (translation) 38
  On Being Someone, 34, 69, 74, 130,
    141
  *What a Piece of Work: On Being
    Human,* 19
Othello, see Shakespeare

Names Index

Oxford Dictionary of the Christian Church, ed. Cross and Livingstone, 152
Pandora, 44
Paul, apostle, 54, 58, 73, 93, 101, 104, 117
  Epistles:
    Colossians, 101
    1 Corinthians, 65, 90, 91, 92, 94, 102, 108, 135, 137
    2 Corinthians, 4, 38f, 62, 132, 142
    Ephesians, 59–60, 94, 101
    Galatians, 45, 117, 125, 133
    Philippians, 48, 138, 149
    Romans, 45, 100, 116, 117, 133, 137, 149
    I Thessalonians, 124
    2 Timothy, 26
Peter, apostle, First Epistle, 17, 33, 66, 94
Pharisees, 122, 135
Pilate, 142
Plato, Euthyphro dialogue, 22
Platten, Stephen, Preface, 109
Plotinus, 103
Polkinghorne, John, 36n6
Price, H. H. Perception, 42 51
Psalms: 9: 64;
  19: 117, 127;
  22: 65, 88, 99;
  33:147;
  34:150;
  37: 65;
  44: 64, 131;
  45: 64;
  48: 12, 47;
  65:16;
  68: 64, 130;
  72: 64;
  74: 26;
  86: 94;
  91: 78;
  92: 8;
  103: 130, 139;
  104: 54;
  118: 60;
  128: 8
"Rabbi Ben Ezra," see Browning

Richard II, see Shakespeare
Robin Hood, 44
Rowell, Geoffrey et al., eds., Love's Redeeming Work, 15
Russell, Bertrand, The Problems of Philosophy, 42, 51
Ryle, Gilbert, The Concept of Mind, 63

Saint Simon, Duc de, 30
Saki (H. H. Munro), 120, quoted by C. S. Lewis, 10
I Samuel, 99
Santa Claus, St Nicholas, Father Christmas, 45
Sartre, Jean-Paul, Huis Clos, 94
Satan, the devil, 30, 35, 63, 64, 99–100
Sayers, Dorothy L., 81,144
Screwtape, see Lewis, C. S.
Shadrach, Meshach & Abednego, 22–23
Shakespeare, William, 7
  As you like it, 8
  Hamlet, 44
  Henry IV Part I, 40
  Henry V, 31
  Julius Caesar, 151–52
  Macbeth, 8
  Measure for measure, 152
  Othello, 58
  Richard II, 7
Shand, John, "A Refutation of the Existence of God," 49
Shaw, G. B., Androcles and the Lion, 56
Solomon, 51
Spirit, see God, Holy Spirit
Spooner, Dr., 43
Stephen, first martyr, 146
Stevenson, Kenneth, see Rowell, et al.
Syro-Phoenician woman, 76

Teilhard de Chardin, Pierre, 9
Tennyson, Alfred, Lord, "Ulysses," 31
Thomas, apostle, 51, 57
Titian 8
Traherne, Thomas, 1, 91
Trinity, see God, Holy Trinity

Ulysses, see Odysseus; "Ulysses," see
   Tennyson

Vanstone, W. H., *Love's Endeavour,
   Love's Expense,* 84
Verdi, 8

Waterloo, battle, 44
Watts, Isaac, 127
Wesley, John, See Butler, Joseph, 17

Williams, Rowan, see Rowell, et al.
Wordsworth, William,
   "Extemporary Effusion Upon the
      Death of James Hogg," 9
   "The Old Cumberland Beggar," 10
   "Ode to Duty," 34, 126
Zebedee, 57
Zeus, 44, 96
Zion, 12, 47

Lightning Source UK Ltd.
Milton Keynes UK
UKOW03f0812130614

233347UK00002B/21/P